Illustrated

CESSNA

BUYER'S ★ GUIDE™

Tom Murphy and Hans Halberstadt

Motorbooks International
Publishers & Wholesalers ®

First published in 1993 by Motorbooks
International Publishers & Wholesalers, PO Box 2,
729 Prospect Avenue, Osceola, WI 54020 USA

Motorbooks International books are also available
at discounts in bulk quantity for industrial or sales-
promotional use. For details write to Special Sales
Manager at the Publisher's address

Library of Congress Cataloging-in-Publication Data
Available

ISBN 0-87938-768-8

Printed and bound in the United States of America

On the front cover: A C-172 takes off from South
County Airport, San Martin, California.

On the back cover: Top, a 1967 O-2A in military
trim, with miniguns and rocket launchers. Many
O-2s are now available on the civilian market,
and buying an O-2A is one of the cheaper ways of
getting into the warbird club. Center, the Citation X
is the fastest business jet on the market, capable of
nearly 600mph top speeds. Bottom, if you're
looking for a taildragger, the C-140 remains one of
the best values on the market. *Peter M. Bowers*

Contents

Introduction

It was a long time ago that I saved up enough money for my first airplane ride. It cost me all of my savings from my paper route, a whole $10—a great deal of money for me at that time. I was having enough trouble figuring out math in the fifth grade without having to come up with the necessary finances to go fly. But I was fascinated with all things aviation and wanted to fly more than anything else. More than sit in school, even.

My parents were like most at that time—dead set against their son setting foot in anything other than the family car, to say nothing about things that left the ground. However, I was dead set on going flying, no matter what happened afterwards. I was going to be a pilot.

There was a small seaplane base about a mile from home. Every day I could see the Grumman and Cessna amphibians lift from Richardson's Bay with a cargo of sightseers. On the side of the base's office building was a sign urging: "See San Francisco From The Air! Only $10!" It seemed as though all I ever did was hang around that place—running to get there after school, coming home late for dinner.

There were a couple of derelict fuselages parked out back that kids like myself used to crawl around on and sit in what was left of the cockpit. We flew those wrecks all over the world. When the real airplanes arrived or departed, I watched them with the same kind of awe and admiration I later felt for certain spectacular young ladies. Both the airplanes and the women were desirable and unobtainable.

As I grew older, I found that both the airplanes and beautiful women were obtainable, after all. But it took initiative, patience, self-confidence, a lot of specialized skill, and more money than I ever thought possible.

Since then, I have been involved with a wide variety of Cessna airplanes. My second flight was in a C-195. I sat on the floor, watched the jumpmaster, and prayed. At 3,000ft, I climbed out on the strut and introduced myself to the thrill of skydiving. I think I made about seven takeoffs before I actually got to see what it was like to land that old Cessna.

Not long after that, I received a letter from my friendly draft board, saying that since I'd registered for the armed services a while ago, they were going to let me come down and meet the Army. Lucky for me, they were short of pilots at that time, so I was able to get into flight school. With visions of air combat and fighter planes running through my mind, I gleefully signed up.

You know what a Cessna L-19/O-1 Bird Dog is? Well, I didn't either, when flight school began. But Fort Rucker, the Army aviation center, managed to rectify that in about six months of intensive training. My flight instructor moonlighted (literally) as a crop

Where it all starts. A Cessna 152 and 172 in the run-up area prior to departure. The 152 (near airplane) holds a student going on his first cross country while working on his private pilot license.

duster. My quest for a pilot's license included some very low-level navigation as well as some of the most interesting cross-country flying I had ever experienced. As we approached the airport to land on some flights, we had to climb in order to be high enough to enter the traffic pattern.

Since those early days, I have had the opportunity to check out a great many types of airplanes, including the T-6 Texan, the P-3 Orion, KC-135 Tanker, the Apache helicopter, and a lot of other interesting aircraft. But most of my time now is in Cessnas. Probably most of your time too.

If you're reading this book, the chances are the first airplane ever to feel your quivering hand on the throttle was a Cessna 152 or one of its variants. Thousands of 152s and 172s have been the first airplane for hundreds of thousands of new pilots. The retractable RGs, the twins, the jets, and the AG planes

have all had a dominant role in the evolution of our flying tradition. It's America's airplane, in a way.

So there are a lot of used airplanes out there. And most of them come up for sale, at one time or another. Making the transition from a renter pilot to an aircraft owner is a big transition—you'll learn more about aviation than at any other time except when you first learned to fly.

If you are thinking about buying an airplane—your first or fifteenth—the same criteria apply. Treat every purchase with the preparation and effort that went into getting your ticket.

People buy airplanes for lots of reasons. It's a good idea to be honest with yourself at the outset about your own motivations.

One common incentive is a simple love of airplanes—the desire to actually possess one independent of actually flying it. The airplanes of these folks can be seen at every airport, some with flat tires, out of annual, neglected. There's one at my airport that actually has a piece of plywood as a door. For each one there is someone who can say at a party or a gathering of pilots, "Sure, I own an airplane." Sometimes just knowing they own something that used to fly is enough for them. Sometimes a restoration project got sidetracked—a new house, new baby, recent shift in marriage arrangements—some reason not to work on the airplane. I was told early in my flying career that to begin an airplane restoration project, you have to be crazy, rich, or about to go through a divorce. Words to live by.

Another reason for ownership is for saving time. Time, to some people, is such a valuable commodity that owning an airplane for the purpose of getting around faster than with a car or other means is justification in itself. You can spend money owning an airplane a lot more easily than you can save money with one, though.

Old aviation joke based in truth:

Question: "What makes an airplane fly?"

Answer: "Money."

You can make money in aviation—not easily, but it can be done.

'Nother joke: "How do you make a small fortune in aviation?"

Answer: "Start with a large one!"

Cessnas do make money—dusting crops, transporting executives, shooting pictures, doing runs as air ambulances, and of course serving as flight-school rentals.

The other end of the spectrum. A nice pair of Cessnas, a 421 Golden Eagle in front of a mint 310.

And finally, an excellent reason for ownership for a new pilot is to build flight time and develop proficiency.

Owners talking:

"If you have a choice of two airplanes—one flying and one sitting—buy the one that's flying."

"I was tired of renting. Getting into an airplane someone else just got out of wasn't my idea of flying. I want control of the plane. I want to know that when I come back to my airplane, it's in the same condition I left it. No candy wrappers, no dog hair, no old torn charts—just what I want in the airplane."

"Honestly? Let me see. I'd have to say one of my main reasons to own an airplane is ego massage. I'm proud to own my Cessna. Sets me above the renter pilots. Is that truthful enough?"

"Ownership is getting very expensive. Only five hundred or so of these things were built last year, and the older ones aren't getting any cheaper to operate. I don't think I've ever been able to afford any airplane I've owned. Gotta want to own one real bad."

"Buying an airplane taught me more about flying than I've ever known. When all the bills had my name on them, everything became more important. All of a sudden, the oil pressure gauge became as important as the altitude indicator."

"No one needs a small airplane—they're mostly expensive toys."

"An airplane is nothing but empty sky, surrounded by aluminum, that you throw money at. No one needs one. But life wouldn't be half as interesting if I didn't own one."

My first trip into the wonderful world of airplane ownership was with a 1967 Piper Cherokee 140. I had been renting new Piper Archers, Warriors, and Cessna 172s for years, so I was used to airplanes that were less than two years old and had low-time airframes and engines. Then I stepped into a fourteen-year-old Cherokee for the grand sum of $10,000. Guess what! Didn't work like the new ones. My education began. If it was to fly, I was the one who was going to have to make it go. I think it taught me more in the two years I owned it than I ever learned in all

Doug Remington, owner of the Flying Country Club fixed base operation (FBO), schedules another pilot for a rental flight. Most pilots begin their careers learning to fly through a club like this.

my previous years of flying other people's airplanes.

Since that first Cherokee, however, I have continued to purchase, repair, restore, and sometimes even fly another eight airplanes, most of them Cessnas. In the process of purchasing these aircraft, I've learned a great deal about each. Back then, there was no handbook for the potential buyer such as you now hold in your hand. I wish that I had had something like this when I first went out Cessna hunting. It would have saved me untold hours of searching and a large amount of money, spent both before I purchased the aircraft and after I owned it. Or I should say, after the plane decided to let me be the next person to throw money at it.

You really have to want to fly to take on the responsibilities of owning an airplane. However, as I said before, purchasing my first airplane taught me more about flying than all the shiny, low-time new planes on lease back down at the big Fixed Base Operator (FBO) where I had been renting airplanes for three years or so. Most of the time, I just picked up the keys, checked the "squawks," walked around a fairly new 172 or Piper, performed a routine preflight, kicked the tires, and lit the fires.

This one's not going anywhere soon. Now that the general aviation fleet is beginning to age, scenes like this are becoming more common as owners of older airplanes in the Cessna 150 and 152 range and up are finding it harder to buy up to larger aircraft, so they resort to major overhaul on what they have.

It took me the better part of two years to figure out that each one of these airplanes had its own logbook, kept under the counter in the FBO's front office, and that it probably would be a good idea to read through it before I took a totally unfamiliar airplane into the sky. Found out the logbook is about as important to the airplane as the radio. I could trace the history of the plane since it rolled out the factory doors at Wichita.

Most of the information that interested me was the last 100 hours of flight time. I could see that all the required inspections had been performed on time and that time-limited parts, such as the battery for the Emergency Locating Transmitter (ELT), were still current. Usually a five- or ten-minute scan of the logbook would be enough for me. Then I'd hand it back to the employee behind the counter and head off to the airplane.

Now that I've become an aircraft owner, I've learned to read the aircraft logbook as though it's my income tax return. I want to know everything that's happened to this particular aircraft since it was new. The aircraft logbook is the single most important document connected with the airplane. Without a logbook, an aircraft is automatically worth 30 percent less, at a minimum, no matter how good it looks. As a matter of fact, I would say that if you are a first-time aircraft buyer, you should avoid like the plague any airplane without a logbook, no matter what the owner says about the condition of the aircraft or how the airplane appears to the eye. I repeat, it is imperative that the logbook be with any aircraft you plan to purchase.

The first step in buying a Cessna or any other used aircraft is to do all the necessary research. Yes, yes, I know you'd much rather spend your time in the cockpit daydreaming about future flights; all the paper shuffling interests you like getting a tetanus shot. But every sale starts with the paperwork. Indubitably the most important part of the purchase. If the paperwork reads like a Grimm Brothers fairy tale (a nice story but having nothing to do with the airplane in front of you), or is full of blank spaces where annuals or 100-hour inspections should be, then my advice to you would be to thank the owner

for his time and cross that one off your list. No paperwork, no purchase.

There are many different publications available that will give you an idea as to the approximate purchase price of the Cessna of your dreams. *Trade-A-Plane* (410 West Fourth Street, Crossville, TN 38557) is probably the best source of current asking prices for any model you might be interested in buying. However, in this financial climate (1993), prices are anything but stable, so I would use price guides as just that—guides. As an example, a friend of mine just recently parted with his C-337 Skymaster after an intense advertising campaign, during which he found that the selling price for Skymasters, in the same relative condition as his, were varying by as much as $10,000 over or under what he was asking for his. What he wanted and what he took home were two very different numbers.

Trade publications and sales sheets will also give you a good idea as to how an average model is equipped with radios and other options such as custom interiors or seating layout. Once you learn how to decipher all the abbreviations, all of the ads will start to make sense to you. It just looks like a different language—it's really English.

If you've narrowed down your choice of aircraft to a particular model, obtain a copy of the operating manual from an airport bookstore or gift shop and read it through several times until you are familiar with what your airplane should look like and how it should perform.

When I bought my first Cessna, a 180 taildragger, model year 1955, I was so new at aircraft ownership that even after having previously owned a Piper Cherokee for over two years, I still barely knew what I was getting into. I hadn't even opened the operating manual before I jumped into the left seat and the owner said, "Let's go shoot some touch-and-gos." About all I knew about that 180 was some hangar stories I'd heard from friends of the owner. Kinda "Go check the gas and oil; the rest of it doesn't matter." That sort of pre-purchase inspection. Not really in-depth research! After I survived the ride ("See, taildraggers ain't that hard to land, now, are they?"), purchased the airplane, and managed to taxi it over to my tiedown, I began to wonder if perhaps I should have handled this whole deal in a slightly different manner. I guess the old saw about "God protecting fools . . . " really worked in my case. However, I didn't get off totally free-and-easy, since I ended up rebuilding all the cylinders after about 50 hours of operation. At an average of $1,100 per! And the Continental engine has six of 'em! Pretty expensive education, don't you think?

Along the same lines of "look before you spend," it would be a good idea to contact a club specifically organized for your airplane. The Cessna Pilots Association (see the appendix for the address) has a monthly newsletter covering all types of piston-engined Cessnas. The newsletter has all the current information and service reports along with features on members' aircraft. Older issues are available. The association will definitely have the most up-to-date information on whatever model you're considering.

Also, the Cessna Tech Center at the Santa Maria, California, Airport, has a training program for owners and potential owners that's very helpful as far as what to look for when doing a pre-purchase inspection on a possible acquisition. The Cessna Tech Center offers a number of classes on what is permitted by the Federal Aviation Administration (FAA) on owner-performed maintenance. The course goes into great detail on the care and feeding of individual models, with instructors working directly with the owners on their own Cessnas. From time to time, the center holds seminars on individual models of Cessnas, with pilots bringing their airplanes to Santa Maria for the weekend. The cost is minimal for the large amount of information an owner can learn through the course.

The FAA has prepared a booklet called *Plane Sense, General Aviation Information*, to acquaint prospective owners with some fundamental information on the requirements of owning and operating a private airplane.

One pilot has gone the route of having his tricycle-geared 152 converted to a taildragger. Sometimes an upgrade to a 150hp engine goes along with the taildragger conversion, makes for a real short takeoff and landing (STOL) aircraft.

This advisory circular (AC 20-5F) can be obtained by writing to the FAA.

Agreed, it's a bit of an effort to try to fish anything out of the great government lake, but in this case the results are definitely worth some of your time and a stamp. For once, it is the government, and they are here to help you.

Last year fewer than six hundred new, single-engined piston airplanes were sold. The existing fleet is tapping twenty years average age. If you figure that seven hundred thousand or more people in the US hold valid pilot's certificates, that works out to not many airplanes for a lot of people. The corollary to this is that the demand for good, low-time airplanes is rising rapidly. When the supply falls, the price will climb. (Econ 101. I did learn something in school.) The product liability brouhaha isn't going to get any better in the foreseeable future. A major engine manufacturer just lost a $105 million lawsuit. Piper is dancing with the bankruptcy attorneys, trying to stay alive. It recently announced that the last shipment of Piper Super Cubs has been weaned from the factory, with no more to come. Actually, Piper says it was making about $1.50 per Super Cub sold, so the profit margin was kind of small.

Cessna's smallest airplane sold with a propeller in 1992 is the 208 Caravan. If you want a new single from Cessna, it will set you back something over $1 million. Cessna also says that if it were to get back into the small airplane game, a C-182 would lighten your wallet by $250,000. Now, I don't know about you, but after paying $21,000 for my last 182 (a 1971 model), a quarter-of-a-million dollars for a new one, providing one is built, seems a tad stiff for me. Let's see: if you put $50,000 down, financing the rest for fifteen years, that would be a payback of $15,000 a year not counting interest. Then you get to pay for the flying. Figure on spreading the cost over 100 hours per year. Probably run around $3,000 a month to fly a 182—if Cessna could be talked into making any more of them, which is doubtful.

So it comes to this. If you plan to buy a used Cessna of any type, don't wait for the current prices to drop. Aircraft, small ones, are the only form of recreational vehicle to continue to escalate in price during this recession. If I were out looking for airplanes instead of writing about them, I'd probably go spend more than I could afford. I could quit buying food. It wouldn't hurt to lose a few pounds—don't need to eat anymore.

Almost everything on the market will have at least 1,000 hours on the tach. A lot of airplanes in most people's price range will have been built in the seventies and have been through an engine or two by now. This is the only game in town where the world's most widely read magazine about the sport features a ten-year-old product on the front cover. They ain't making them like they used to. As a matter of fact, they ain't making them at all. Now—not in a year or two—is the time to buy an airplane.

In another life, mayhaps the world is filled with new light airplanes that cost about what a top line car such as a Ferrari or Porsche would run, but not here on this planet. I don't foresee a time coming in the next ten years when airplanes will drop in price.

Aviation has never been cheap. You can't have a paper route and afford airplanes. I don't think that I was ever able to afford any of the airplanes that I owned, but I surely did enjoy them.

If you succumb to the aviation drug, you will find it to be the strongest addiction imaginable. The thought of flying down to the Bahamas will make your fingers clench an imaginary yoke in anticipation. Checking out a new airplane will raise your excitement quotient into the overload zone. And going on your instrument check ride will wring you out like a used bar towel.

I don't know of any other occupation or sport where you can sit still and sweat so much. Or have so much fun. This is the only game I've played in which I was scared spitless and grinning at the same time.

This is a book that covers buying a used Cessna aircraft. What's in the market. What to look for. What type of airplane to buy. But this book doesn't take the place of the Pilot's Operating Handbook (POH) for whatever airplane you are purchasing. The POH is the

This 152 really shows that it has spent its life as a trainer. Some 152s have over 11,000 hours on them. It used to be that the airplane turned into parts at the 5,000–6,000hr range, but with no more being made, you just keep rebuilding what you have.

authority; I'm the opinion. In no way do I pretend that everything about used Cessnas is between these two covers. If it were, lifting the book would require special equipment.

The purpose of this book is to provide information to people who have at least a rudimentary knowledge of airplanes. If you don't have a pilot's license, or are in the beginning throws of learning which part of the airplane stays upright, then some of the book won't be totally clear.

Buy it anyway. Couple of reasons. One, you just might be in the airplane market in a few years, and the information in here, other than prices, will still be current. Two, if you buy this book, I might be able to afford another airplane again. It will be another Cess-

na too. I've owned a few, and thoroughly enjoyed each one.

I spent a lot of time learning about that first C-180. I bought it back when gas was cheap and all airports had a waiting list for tiedowns.

Once my name was on the title, I was responsible for everything that happened to the aircraft. Took me a while to figure out what that meant. The first annual made everything crystal clear. When I bought the 180, the annual inspection was just about due, so the seller knocked off a chunk of the asking price, and I did the annual in lieu of a pre-purchase. This wasn't as scary as it sounds. The previous owner agreed to pay for any major problems that appeared if I sprung for the annual.

Sounded like a deal to me. Money changed hands. I owned an airplane. Now what?

Time for the annual. I figured that some money could be saved if I did some of the grunt work on the airplane, while leaving the actual inspection to the mechanic. The first way I saved money was to go buy a battery-operated drill with two extra batteries and a charger. The way it works is that you either own an electric screw gun or you end up with arms like Popeye. Then I bought some screwdrivers and specialty wrenches from my friendly Snap-On man. $263.45. Boy—we're saving money now! So much for cheap.

A word about tools. If you plan to work on your airplane, doing all the repairs and maintenance allowed by the FAA, don't go cheap on tools. Round off a few screws with a low-buck Phillips screwdriver, maybe bust off a few heads and have to drill them out, and then you'll see the wisdom of buying good tools. If it was cheap and would work, the FBO would have it. All the wrench twisters that I've dealt with buy good stuff. I didn't; I learned; now I do.

When you take the airplane apart for the first time, go buy a stainless steel screw set to put it back together. A complete screw kit, including a few spares to replace the ones you lose, can be found in any airport shop. Or you can mail order a kit out of *Trade-A-Plane* for under $40, unless your Cessna is a 421. That kit will run $109.75 at last glance. Next time you have to open up an inspection plate, you will see the wisdom of these words. Plus, if you keep the airplane for a while—say ten years or so—stainless screws make real good sense.

See how much money we're saving by helping on the annual. Much more savings like this and it's time for a second job. But knowledge never comes inexpensively.

Most of the bits and pieces needed for that first annual can be used down the line as future maintenance becomes necessary, so it's not like this happens every time. Plus things like stainless steel screws will make it easier and faster the next time. See how much fun you are having. Haven't even got to the flying stuff yet.

Well, after much weeping and gnashing of teeth, the 180 went back together. Next it was time to go turn gasoline into noise.

First, though, insurance had to be found. On the phone I went. Called a lot of brokers, got the same answer. I needed 250 hours total time (TT), 15 hours instruction in type, and 15 hours solo before they would cover me. And they meant fifteen, not almost fifteen or close to fifteen. Mostly this was due to my total lack of taildragger time. On a tricycle gear the requirements would probably be less.

Turns out that the 15 hours instruction were needed. Any one who says that flying a taildragger is simple, is simple. Boy, I never had an airplane try to go in more different directions at the same time as I did with that Cessna 180. My foibles with it are covered in greater detail in Chapter Two.

Well, I got my Cessna running and legal for another year, got checked out in it and insured. I was flying my own airplane. Now what about the airplane that you're going to buy?

That's what this book is all about—buying a used Cessna. What's up for sale, what to look for, what it might take to make it fly, and a few hard learned hints to help you stay out of the thorns. If this book helps you buy an airplane, then it's served its purpose.

I hope you have as much fun reading this as I did writing it.

But hope it doesn't take as long.

Tom Murphy
San Jose, California
April 1993

Investment Rating

All the airplanes in this book are rated in three categories using numbers 1 through 5 (1 being the most desirable and 5 being the least desirable). The categories are:

Investment
Utility
Popularity

If it's a 3, it's average in the category. You see a 5—not a chance; you lose. A 1 rating on your dream machine—go for it; live life like a beer commercial.

However, remember that these ratings are based on opinions of pilots I've interviewed and on my own experiences. If you have found the airplane of your dreams, far be it from me to dissuade you from owning it. This is only a guide to Cessnas—nothing in it is engraved in stone.

And, at all times, the POH is the final authority on all aircraft. Consult it before making any flights in any airplane. Above all, have fun.

Chapter 1

The Early Birds 1911–1945

This first chapter could have been entitled "Scarcity and Rarity" just as easily as anything else, since there aren't a whole lot of pre-World War II Cessna airplanes on the market. Those that do turn up from time to time are not the type of airplane that you would use for day-to-day flying.

Models such as the T-50 twin are quite rare, even though they were built by the hundreds in many different variations in both civilian and government models.

About the only way to find some of the early models would be to frequent antique airshows or join a group that specializes in a specific model of Cessna. One good place to start looking for the Cessna T-50 is with the Cessna T-50 Flying Bobcats. Other clubs you should contact include the Cessna Airmaster Club, and the Cessna Owner Organization. (Addresses for these and other clubs can be found in the appendix.)

Since this is supposed to be a buyer's

One of the first Cessna T-50s. Used by the Civil Aeronautics Authority (CAA) back when tail numbers had an NC prefix. *Peter M. Bowers photo*

Clyde Cessna's Silverwing at Cherokee, Oklahoma, summer 1911. *Cessna Aircraft Company/ Peter M. Bowers*

guide, going back to how Clyde Cessna spent his waking hours flogging fabric and whipping wires into the first 1911 Queen Monoplane is beyond its scope. Mainly because the only Queen monoplane that you'll ever find for sale will be fifteen inches long and powered by rubber bands.

The first few airplanes that most people could reasonably expect to find for sale, in a price range from cheap to about that of a good Ferrari, will be covered here. Not that any of these airplanes can be found down at the local FBO. But who knows? You might get lucky.

In some sort of order, here are a few pre-1945 Cessnas that might be found for sale.

First is the Model AA, approved August 1928. It has a Cessna Modified Anzani 120hp radial engine and a Hamilton wood pro-

peller. It has a 40ft, 2in wingspan, is 25ft, 6in long, with a height of just over 7ft. Empty weight is 1,304lb; gross runs 2,260lb. It carries 40gal of fuel, which leaves 510lb for payload. Maximum speed is 120mph, cruise speed is 102mph, and landing speed is 45mph. A total of fifteen Model AAs were built from 1927 to 1929 at a cost to the public of $5,750. Probably not more than one or two left in the world. Might be hard to find one to restore.

Next comes the Cessna Model AW. Cessna built a whole bunch of these airplanes between 1928 and 1930—forty-eight to fifty. Looks similar to the Model AA, with a Warner 110hp radial engine.

The specs are just about the same as those for the Model AA except the AW, with the Warner Scarab engine, makes the AW about 8mph faster in top end and 3mph in cruise. It will cover another 80 miles at that blistering cruise on the same amount of fuel, for a total range of 630 miles. Not bad for an airplane built before your father knew what airplanes were.

It sold new for $6,900 in 1928, later climbing to $7,500. To put this into perspective, remember a new 1928 Packard was bringing down $2,275 for the loss leader model, while $4,400 would get a high-dollar Clipper. And Packard was the kind of car that only advertised in *National Geographic*. Gives a good idea as to how airplane prices compared to cars back then.

So the Cessna Model AW was an expensive toy back in the late '20s. Possibilities of finding one are right up there with having the IRS send you money. Could happen, but not likely.

Anzani powered Model A prototype with an airframe load of seventeen men in 1927—a good Cessna publicity stunt. *Cessna Aircraft Company/Peter M. Bowers*

The welded frame and landing gear of a Model AW. If you look at a newer Citabria or a 1993 Tay-lorcraft F-22, you'll see that things haven't changed much. *Cessna Aircraft Company/Peter M. Bowers*

The Model AW is not quite as scarce as the Model AA, but I've never seen either one for sale, and if I did, someone else would have just bought it. Maybe you.

In 1929, Cessna got a Type Certificate for the Model DC-6. (No, it's not a small DC-3; has nothing to do with Douglas Aircraft.) This is a larger aircraft than the early AA and AW models, with a bigger cabin and a Curtiss six-cylinder radial pumping out 170hp.

The wingspan is 40ft, 8in, with a mean aerodynamic chord of 78in. The total weight is 2,988lb. Empty, it's 1,767, so the payload, with 66gal of fuel, is 633lb. At 10gph, the DC-6 will cover 575 miles at a cruise speed of 105mph, landing at 48mph.

Only five were built, and Curtiss Flying Service bought all five. Four were later converted to Wright-radial power.

Maybe you can buy a picture of one. Most likely you can't buy the airplane itself, though who knows what lurks out there in used-airplane land.

Cessna then went to the Model DC-6A. Just over twenty of this model were built. This is a lot more airplane than the DC-6. The 6A has a Wright nine-cylinder radial, reaching 300hp at 2,000rpm. The gross weight is

3,350lb. Useful load is 1,250lb. Total fuel is 66gal, feeding the Wright at 13gph.

The best part is the cruise speed. With 300 horses to drag a little more than a ton-and-a-half of fabric and tubing through the air, the DC-6A runs along at 130mph. Top end is 160mph. Plus, lightly loaded, it will do the old "homesick angel" climb at 1,300fpm. This is pretty good when compared to the Ford Trimotor, which had the same cruise speed. It was powered by three 300hp Wrights, and had all it could do to go upstairs at 950fpm.

In September 1929, just in time for the biggest depression that America had ever seen, Cessna brought out the Model DC-6B. It had pretty much the same airframe as the DC-6A, but with a Wright 225hp radial replacing the 300hp engine. The same number of 6Bs and 6As were built—twenty-two. The 6B had a gross weight of 3,100lb (250lb less than the 6A), but the payload stayed the same.

Seventy-five fewer horses gave the 6B a slightly slower cruising speed. Not much less, though. Count on burning 11gph for a 120mph ride over 685 miles.

Cessna DC-6B. The DC-6 was approved September 1929 and was powered by a 225hp Wright radial. This one went to Curtiss Flying Service of Texas. *Cessna Aircraft Company/Peter M. Bowers*

This was Cessna's flagship C-37, as can be seen on the logo on the tail. The C-37 first flew December 1936 with Duane Wallace at the controls. Wallace helped Cessna survive the Great Depression by riding the bus to Washington, D.C., to deal with the CAA. *Cessna Aircraft Company/Peter M. Bowers*

All of the DC-6 models had fairly roomy cabins, upholstered with the same material found in quality cars of the day. The panel, compared to what is in the average C-172 today, looks as bare as a plain sheet of cardboard. Remember, though, not only were there no radios installed in airplanes in those days, but also there was no one on the ground to talk to. You just looked outside to see where you were going. Sounds strange, doesn't it? No TCAs, no ARSAs, no GCA approaches to landing. Nothing but what you saw. Must have been fun.

Anyway, having the bottom fall out of the stock market in October 1929 didn't do much for the Cessna Aircraft Company and the DC-6. As major industries went down the tubes with frightening regularity, accompanied by the patter of bankrupt feet stepping out of office windows, Cessna scaled down, trying to survive and keep the doors open. Stock that had been bringing over $100 per share dropped like a bent duck, finally leveling off below $10. This put the kibosh on DC-6 production, since you'd have had to sell a lot of apples on the street corner to make the over $10k price.

However, some of these airplanes are still floating around. I've heard of one for sure—mayhaps two—being restored.

I think if a Cessna DC-6B figured in my plans, I would take a trip to Oshkosh for the annual fly-in and air show. If any of these things are flying, the proud owners will take them there. Sometimes they even try to sell the airplane at the show.

Remember, a lot of money, labor, and an ex-wife or two has gone into making a DC-6B fly. Don't expect to find it at K-mart prices.

In June 1935, Cessna received the Type Certificate for the C-34. Just forty-two were built in the 1935-36 production run, and few

A C-165 with an experimental X-250 aircraft engine developed by General Motors in 1940. Note the elongated engine cowling. *Cessna Aircraft Company/Peter M. Bowers*

of those remain today. Cruise speed, powered by a Warner seven-cylinder, 145 hp radial, was 143mph with the engine turning slightly more than 1,900rpm. The wingspan was 34ft, 2in. Length was 24ft, 8in. Height was 7ft, 3in.

It weighed 1,380lb empty and could carry a useful load of 980lb, including 35gal of fuel. Range was 550 miles with the engine leaned out to 5gph. It would climb at 800fpm at sea level, returning to land at 47mph with full flaps.

The C-37 and C-38 were basically the same airplane as the C-34; most of the changes involved widening the cabin another 4in at the front wing fittings, which tapered to a 2in increase at the rear of the door. Forty-six of the C-37s and sixteen of the C-38s were assembled before the end of production in 1938. The C-37 was approved for Edo floats in 1937. Part of the approval involved spinning the seaplane six turns in both directions with a one-and-one-half turn recovery. The C-37 passed the testing with ease, going on to prove rock steady in flight.

The C-38 was the first of the series to be called Airmaster, the name now associated with all the Cessnas from the C-34 to the C-165. The C-38 differed from its earlier relations by having a single belly flap instead of the usual arrangement of flaps mounted on each wing. The belly flap actually served more as a speed brake than as a flap, since it provided no lift, just drag. By the time the C-38 came out of the factory, its base price was $6,490. The addition of floats brought the price up to the $10,000 mark. Remember, this was during the time when you could book a 128-day world cruise on Canadian Pacific's Empress of Britain for $2,300. The ship offered five meals a day and numerous land excursions; it was replete with tennis and squash courts and air-conditioned cabins. Flying Cessnas took money then, just as it does today.

In 1938 Cessna's engineers came up with an improved version of the C-38, calling it the C-145 Airmaster, along with a slightly faster model, the C-165, which cruised along at 157mph on 165hp. Almost eighty of the C-145/165 series were built until World War II put a stop to production.

All of the Airmaster series exhibited the stability at all speeds and the light controls for which Cessna had a reputation. Except for heavy elevator pressure below 75mph on final, requiring that a lot of trim be cranked in on approach, flying the Airmasters required little work. They could be trimmed to fly hands-off as long as the air was smooth.

By the time the last few C-165s passed down the assembly line, the model had been in production for seven years. Something faster was needed for a new airplane capable of packing five people at the 200mph range. Thus was born Cessna's first production twin, the T-50 Bobcat.

In 1939 Cessna expanded its product line to include a low-wing, twin-engined, retractable-geared, 185mph-top-speed airplane called the T-50, probably because it was the fiftieth type design the company engineered.

The T-50's two Jacobs seven-cylinder radials produced a total of 450hp while turning 2,000rpm. It had a range of 850 miles, burning 27gph. Fuel capacity was 120gal standard with an optional 160gal available. Even as a 170mph cruising airplane, it could be hauled down to 55mph with the flaps extended, so landing on short, unimproved airstrips wasn't a problem.

A total of forty of these planes were built from 1939–42, with the price starting at $29,675. The company still struggled along trying to cover expenses, building small numbers of airplanes and pushing hard to make the payroll. They counted themselves lucky when they only lost a little over $1,000 for a four-month period in 1939.

Then something came along to change Cessna's and all the world's fortunes: World War II. Since this isn't a history book, I'll stick to Cessna's manufacture of the AT-8, Cranes, UC-78, and the AT-17 in all their various guises. All the Advanced Trainers (AT) that Cessna built for the military, here and in Canada, were variations on the original T-50 Twin. Various modifications were incorporated until production ceased in 1944, when the Allies looked to be on the winning path. For our purposes, we'll consider all the aircraft to be similar.

Coming in! A Royal Canadian Air Force T-50 Crane checks out another student. These aircraft were delivered to the armed forces by the thousands to act as twin-engine trainers. They were built until 1944, when production was terminated. *Peter M. Bowers*

Finding an AT-17 in good flying condition is not the easiest of tasks. From what I could discover, any aircraft for sale has been totally taken apart, the main spar either x-rayed or dye-checked or both, motors rebuilt a few times, all fabric replaced. These are only slightly rarer than F-104 Starfighters. For a first project or warbird restoration, you would be far better off with a single-engined Cessna such as the O-1 or T-41 Mescalero (the 172 in military colors). If you have experience in doing fabric work and rebuilding tube and wood airplanes, go ahead. Just remember how these things were flown by nineteen-year-old pilots, trying to learn how to fly a twin. They are tough airplanes, but they are also fifty years old and have had very hard lives. Expect to spend an inordinate amount of money to make one fly. With so many other military projects waiting to soak up money, I'd say that unless you have some sentimental reason to own one (say you were born in the back of an AT-17), give this airplane a pass.

Early Cessna Rating: Since all the pre-1945 Cessnas are in collector status, rating them other than as investments is rather hard.

Investment: Whatever the collector market will bear. Don't buy just to make money—you probably won't.

Utility: All aircraft—#5
Popularity: C-145/165—#2
AT-17—#4
AW—#5
AA—#5
C-34 and C-38—#4
DC-6—#5

Chapter 2

The Taildraggers

Back in 1945 a strange thing happened to World War II: peace was declared!

Everybody got to pack up their toys of destruction and begin to get on with the rest of their lives. With all the technological advances brought about in aviation during World War II, airplanes had taken a mighty jump forward.

Now that all the B-17s, B-29s, and P-51s were being turned into frying pans, and all the troops were on their way back to the good ole USA and a better life, manufacturers were finally able to start producing all the goodies that had been gracing the pages of *Life* and *National Geographic* magazines for the last couple of years.

Most aircraft companies figured that there wouldn't be much demand for a Boeing B-29 heavy bomber, replete with functional .50cal machine-guns, so Cessna went ahead with plans to produce something on a slightly smaller scale. Not many could afford the care and feeding that it took to keep an ex-World War II aluminum tank in the air, so the rush was on to produce something on a slightly smaller scale—like the series of light planes that had been on the drawing board towards the end of hostilities. Although a P-51 Mustang could be purchased from the Military Aircraft Disposal Board for less than $5,000, its utility was somewhat restricted on a cross-country flight. A more practical solution was needed. (Although had I known then what I know now, I'd probably have tried to spend the bread money for a Mustang, Thunderbolt, or Hellcat. Bread money in those days was around five figures—$100.00. Probably woulda' taken a while to save the money, even if I had given up eating.)

C-190 and C-195

At one time Cessna had developed a "Family Car of the Air" to be built after peace descended. But that idea went by the board in favor of a newer design known as P-780.

This airplane was to use as many as possible of the existing T-50 bits and pieces while still resembling the C-145/C-165 Airmaster

A rare shot of a Cessna 195 on floats. Additional vertical stabilizers were added to the tail for stability when floats were mounted. *Peter M. Bowers*

singles. The new airplane, soon to be called the C-190, had a larger cabin than the Airmaster, and the strut landing gear was replaced by Cessna's new spring steel assemblies. The first airplane was powered by a Jacobs 245hp radial engine with a second prototype fitted with a Jacobs ("Shaky-Jake") 300hp engine that pushed the all-aluminum 190 to almost 180mph down on the deck.

Finally Cessna decided to produce both airplanes—the C-190 with a 240hp Continental radial engine and the C-195 fitted with the 300hp Jacobs. Back in 1947 Cessna sold a total of eighty-four C-190s and C-195s. Not a bad start for a new design. In 1948, sales hit 205, which turned out to be the high-water mark as far as selling airplanes went.

To give an example of what post-World War II pilots had to contend with in the C-190 series, Time Between Overhaul (TBO) recommended for the Jacobs radial was 800 hours. You could count yourself among the blessed if all the cylinders functioned for the whole 800 hours without the attentions of a machine shop. Usually when the oil consumption got totally out of hand (one to two quarts per

hour), it was time to pull the jugs. But this wasn't considered unusual for an engine built in the fifties. The military staff at that time weren't getting much, if any, more time out of their Wrights and Pratt & Whitney big radials. The Boeing B-17 bomber had four 1,200hp Wright nine-cylinder radials powering it. At one point, the mechanics were lucky to get 200 hours on an engine before it came apart. Course, having to dodge flak and Messerschmitt Bf 109s probably didn't do much for longevity, either. Anyway, at 800 hours, off came the Cessna's engine.

Things were going well for Cessna, selling 186 airplanes in 1949 and 190 in 1950. So far, the new airplane was a success. Cessna not only had a good-looking, good-flying, fast airplane, but also had a popular, four-place airplane. Everybody was happy.

Improvements followed, including an interior upgrade, hanging a spinner on the nose, and installing an R-755 Jacobs radial in 1952 when the C-195B made its appearance. Because of declining sales (fewer than a hundred in 1953), Cessna elected to discontinue the 190. The C-195 was soon to follow its smaller brother in 1954 when customers stayed away in droves.

During the eight-year life of the C-190 series, the Air Force took a liking to the airplane, buying fifteen C-195s and calling them model LC-126A. These served their time in the military playing in the snow up in the far north. Compared to the civilian version, the LC-126 was equipped with the usual military radios, was painted accordingly, and was fitted with pretty stark interiors.

In 1952 the Army got into the game, buying sixty-three C-195s, called LC-126Cs, to use as a flying ambulance. The interiors were reconfigured to handle two stretchers. The baggage doors had to be resized to make them big enough to get the patients in and out.

Including all the military versions, a total of 233 C-190s and 866 of the various 195s were built from 1947–1954. Attrition and wrecks have whittled this number down considerably, so finding a C-190 or C-195 is going to be a bit of a problem.

Most of the remaining airplanes have been through at least one reincarnation,

---

C-190 and C-195 Specifications

Engine, C-190: Continental seven-cylinder radial of 240hp
Engine, C-195: Jacobs seven-cylinder radial of 300hp
Maximum Weight: 3,350lb
Fuel Capacity: 80gal
Maximum Speed, C-190: 170mph
Maximum Speed, C-195: 180mph
Maximum Cruise, C-190: 150mph
Maximum Cruise, C-195: 159mph
Range: 700–725 miles at 13.9gph and 16gph
Rate of Climb, C-190: 1,050fpm
Rate of Climb, C-195: 1,135fpm
Landing Speed with Flaps: 60mph
Service Ceiling, C-190: 16,000ft
Service Ceiling, C-195: 18,300ft
Empty Weight, C-190: 2,030lb
Empty Weight, C-195: 2,050lb
Useful Load, C-190: 1,320lb
Useful Load, C-195: 1,300lb
Payload with 80gal Fuel: 633lb
Length, C-190: 27ft, 2in
Length, C-195: 27ft, 4in
Wing Span: 36ft, 2in
Height: 7ft, 2in

Judging by the antennas on the wings, this C-140 has had its electrical system updated to modern radios. The C-120 and C-140 look nearly identical, but the 120 was not equipped with flaps or rear-quarter windows.

sometimes two. The ones that haven't been restored are generally in such condition that only wishful thinking or about twenty pounds of hundred dollar bills will get them in the air again.

A recent issue of *Trade-A-Plane* shows eleven C-195s for sale. The low asking is $37,000, the high being $78,900 for a freshly restored, fully equipped down-to-the-wheel-covers C-195 with no year specified.

Actually the year of a 195 isn't as important as its condition. All these airplanes are at least forty years old anyway, so what's been done, and by whom, is more important.

Most of the flying 195s have fairly current radios and navigation gear. Four of the airplanes are advertised as fully equipped for IFR (Instrument Flight Rules) operation, with modern radios such as King KX-155s in the panel. I, personally, might be a little hesitant to take a four-decade-old airplane out in hard instrument conditions, but then what do I know?

Arnold Senterfitt, the author of Airports of Mexico and Central America, flew a C-195 all over the world. He specialized in going to some of the remotest landing strips to be found in Mexico. He said his C-195, N1537D, taught him much about flying as he took it through Mexico, with a few trips to Belize thrown in, over thirteen years. He was particularly happy with having an aisle between the front seats and a quiet cruise of 1,800rpm. However, he finally got tired of having to carry 4gal of oil with him on an extended trip and not being able to see much in front of the airplane. So he let his "big old pussycat" go. (Must have been a different 195 than the ones I flew.) His next aerial mule was a Cessna 180, and after he got over being able to see outside, he really went places. His book covers trips to Central America, Panama, and Columbia, making round-trips of 55 hours in the process. I had the pleasure of flying with him to the Meling Ranch in the mountains of Baja California for my fortieth birthday, landing on a one-way runway with a mountain at the other end. Quite a party. Quite a man.

When looking at a C-195 for purchase (we'll skip the C-190, which is doubly rare and mostly similar to a 195), all the rules about pre-purchase inspections apply, as with other airplanes. However, you'd probably be much better off to try for an annual, with the owner paying for the repairs.

The Blue Book prices run all the way from a high of $77,900 for a 1954 model in pristine condition to a low of $32,600 for a 1947 C-195 in average shape. So as you can see, even old 195s still bring a lot of money. They cost a lot of money to operate, too.

It's very important that you contact a club such as the International 195 Club (P.O. Box 737, Merced, CA 95344) before handing over large dollars.

For the really adventurous pilot, *Trade-A-Plane* lists a couple of "projects," disassembled or otherwise, in the $20,000 range. If you're a first-time buyer who doesn't want to fly for a while and whose Gold Card needs stretching, by all means go for it. See you in two or three years. Maybe. If you think it's easy getting boxfuls of 195 up flying, and on floats to boot, you're way beyond needing this book. Call me and let me know how it went.

If I really had the droolies for a C-195, could really see myself behind that big ol' radial, spitting oil and rattling my teeth, I'd go join the club first. Then go play airport bum for a few months. Go wander through a few airports and look at what's tied down. Granted, most of the 195s will be parked in a hangar, probably with a carpeted floor, lights, and even a chrome drip pan under the engine. (Remember what was said above about oil leaks?) You would be fairly safe in figuring this thing is treated well. Not for sale either, I imagine, but that's not the point.

I haven't yet met the aircraft owner who, on a sunny weekend, wouldn't take the time to talk to you about his pride and joy. After all, even though pilots don't have big egos, most can be coerced into talking about the airplane with a little arm twisting. Might even be able to go for a ride if some gas money changes hands. You'll learn more about a C-195 in one hour of flight than in all the books ever to cross your path.

Plus, you'll have a damn good time in the process.
C-190 and C-195 Rating
Investment: #3
Utility: #4
Popularity: #4

Cessna 120 and 140

Back in 1945 after peace had been declared at the end of World War II, the US government offered the returning GIs financial aid to further their education and help them find a career after five years of playing trooper in strange places.

Cessna saw that flight instruction and flight schools would be a fast-growing market for training pilots under the GI Bill. The demand for training aircraft was going to grow far in excess of that during the 1930s. Newer and better training airplanes would have to be designed and built.

Cessna decided to go after its share of

C-120 and C-140 Specifications

Engine, C-120: Continental C-85-12 of 85hp with 1,800-hour TBO
Engine, C-140: Continental C-90-12 of 90hp with 1,800-hour TBO
Maximum Weight: 1,450lb
Fuel Capacity: 25gal
Maximum Speed, C-120: 123mph
Maximum Speed, C-140: 120mph
Range: 420 miles at 5.9gph
Cruising Speed, C-120: 106mph
Cruising Speed, C-140: 105mph
Rate of Climb: 640fpm
Service Ceiling: 15,500ft
Landing Speed, C-120: 42mph
Landing Speed with Flaps, C-140: 40mph
Empty Weight, C-120: 785lb
Empty Weight, C-140: 860lb
Useful Load, C-120: 665lb
Useful Load, C-140: 590lb
Wing Span, C-120 and C-140: 32ft, 10in
Wing Span, C-140A: 33ft, 4in
Length: 21ft, 6in
Height: 6ft, 3in

the market in 1946 with an all-new two-seat aircraft based around a small four-cylinder Continental engine of 85hp.

The fuselage was of all-metal construction, but the strutted wing was still fabric covered to save weight. It also helped that a bedsheet wing was cheaper to build, and that Cessna had been doing it that way for many a year. You get a little new, you get a little old. Sure worked, though. Cessna had a real tough time punching out airplanes fast enough for the dealers standing in line and the customers breathing down the dealer's necks. All for the heady sum of $3,495. Yes, Amelia, the good old days are truly gone forever. Thirty-five hundred dollars in 1946 money was a whole group of dollars, but compare it to what a new trainer would cost in 1993 midget money dollars. Probably couldn't walk out of your local Cessna Airplane-a-Torium for less than $75,000. And it would come with a 350-page book full of disclaimers. And two hungry lawyers in close formation.

As an aside. Do you know why you bury

A vacuum horn on a Cessna 120. The venturi action of the ram air produced enough vacuum to operate the gyros on the directional instruments. No vacuum pump was fitted, nor was a starter or flaps.

lawyers twelve feet down instead of six?

Cause deep down, they are really good people.

All kidding aside folks, product liability games are one of the reasons that the only Cessna aircraft that you can buy new today burns kerosene and costs $900,00 for the loss-leader.

The model 140 became such a popular airplane that Cessna had to put on more people to handle the up to thirty-per-day production in the summer of 1946. If the last 120/140 convention I attended is any indicator, the popularity hasn't dropped a bit. I think spending a warm night sleeping under the wing of your shiny restored C-140 would

be reason enough to go out and buy one. Well, it's easier than sleeping under the wing of a Piper Cherokee. Every time I sat up ... bang ... sore head.

Looking through the trade's papers and advertising pamphlets that float across my desk, the C-140 seems to be running around $12,000. For your investment you get a plane that's been through a complete restoration at least once. Most of them have radios and gear that wasn't even wishful thinking when the airplane was new.

I found a 1947 C-140 with 2,396 hours TT, a nice King radio, transponder/encoder, intercom, and new fabric. Plus it had lived in a hangar since restoration. Came with all logs

Powered by a 85hp Continental four-cylinder engine, this Cessna 140 could blast to 110mph and cruise at 100mph. The factory was turning out twenty-two C-120s and 140s per day in 1946.
Peter M. Bower

since new. All this going for the princely sum of $13,500 or offer. Hmmmm! Excuse me for a minute; I gotta go make a call.

A nice thing about the original production run of C-140s is that if the plane was a little high for your budget at $3,500 a copy, you could go get in line for a low-buck Cessna 120 that was almost an exact copy of the 140, just with some of the frills left off.

What you didn't get on a C-120 were small things like flaps and rear quarter-windows. There was no custom radio panel either. They wouldn't have worked anyway; the C-120 wasn't equipped with an electrical system.

Not having a set of flaps isn't such a large deal on an airplane that lands at moped speeds. But not having an electrical system could definitely pose a problem flying in today's airspace. Although there was a story in one of the past flying mags about a pilot who went all the way across the United States without an electron to his name. Hand propped and all.

By now, most owners have installed at least one nav-com and a Mode C transponder in the panel of their airplanes. Just the minimum needed to enjoy a flight around the countryside with a return to a tower-controlled airport.

The C-140 has now become a collector aircraft, its training days long over. It's the perfect airplane for you and another to pack a lunch on a sunny summer day, go find a dirt airstrip within one to two hours of flying time, and enjoy a day looking outside the airplane as the world slowly moves past.

Speaking of moving past, the book says that the 140 will burn a hole through the sky at almost 105mph, but you want to listen to the weather people when they talk winds. Especially if the wind's coming from where you're going.

A few years ago I took a lady I wished to impress with my flying prowess out for a ride in a friend's C-140. I didn't call for the wind forecast and found myself flying into a real healthy headwind, right on the nose. Didn't impress the lady by moving slowly enough to read the signs on the trucks that passed us. Bad idea. Sure covered ground

when I did a 180 for home, though. Whoosh. Wait for nice, sunny, low-wind days!

If you have the opportunity to watch a 140 or 120 take off into a strong wind, it'll prove to be very educational. The airplane looks like it's riding a slow elevator up. Not much forward motion, just altitude. I wonder, if the headwind were strong enough and if you hung in the air long enough, could you land on the same runway from which you just took off? How would you log that one?

As discussed above, most of the C-120 and C-140 airplanes will have been restored by the time you go looking for one. Some of them will be in better shape than when they flew out of Wichita for the first time.

Some things to watch. If the fabric on the wings is fairly new and is Ceconite or similar cloth, it should give you at least ten years without problems. That's provided it was doped and painted properly. A lot of the 140s have had their wings covered with metal, which solves the fabric problem completely. The model C-140A came out with aluminum wing skins in 1949 and changed the dual wing struts to a singular. If you felt the need for speed, the 85hp Continental could be bypassed and a screaming 90hp substituted in its place. Really smokin' now. Same rated cruise, just got off the ground a little easier.

Costs. We always seem to get to the part that's tough.

At least the 140 won't cost what a 210 does to fly. Cooking along at 5.9gal per 80 to 90 miles across the ground is a fairly inexpensive way to fly.

The engine seems to run forever. And pistons and parts to rebuild the 90hp Continental don't require a second mortgage; just about any licensed mechanic can put one together. Or, if you feel ambitious, you could roll your own, with someone checking as you progress and finally signing it off for you. That would be a fairly inexpensive way to go if you're running on a tight budget.

I saw an 85hp Continental that had been taken off a 120 about two weeks ago. The owner said he'd been picking up metal for the last three or four oil changes, so he figured it was time for a teardown. (For those of you who don't know, metal in the oil screen means you will have a dead engine, real quick. Don't fly for "three or four oil changes" if you find crunchies in the oil. They came from somewhere.)

There was enough metal to fill an oil bottle cap in the screen of the engine, so I thought it would be informative to play watch and see. I thought that when the cases were opened, the crank and rods would show wear. Wrong. Not that good. The crank journals were so far gone that the engine must have rattled like a handful of rocks in an oil drum. Nothing was touching where it was supposed to. You could actually see daylight between the rod and the crank pin. These parts were too far gone to use as paperweights, and this idiot was flying it like this. Oh well. Just turn up the radio. It covers up all those nasty noises.

We estimated that the engine hadn't been apart for 3,000–4,000 hours, or else the guy had flown it on a mixture of cutting oil and sand. I mean, the prop could be moved almost one inch from side to side. No, it didn't get rebuilt. I think the crank turned into a door stop. Shows why you pay the money to look before you pay the money to buy.

By now the 140 has been around long enough for all the big problems to have been ironed out. What has to be watched are the usual bits and pieces that you look for on any forty-year-old airplane. After wading through the logs and finally getting to the airplane, look for corrosion inside the wings and tailfeathers. Find out how many times the engine cases and crank have been rebuilt. Are they on their second go-around, or have they been through three or four life cycles? Parts are parts. Any piece that has been rebuilt once stands a far better chance of staying together than one that has been apart so many times that the edges are taking a polish.

Contact the International Cessna 120/140 Association (address in the appendix). Join the club. There's no better way to learn more about your particular fixation than hanging around with a group of people with the same hobbies. Plus they usually have the inside track on who's selling what and how good a restoration was done.

Trust me. (Sure, Tom!) If your plan is to fly a C-120 or C-140, and you want it to flash in the sunlight at fly-ins, then go out and buy the best one you can almost afford. You can't do the work as cheaply as you can buy all the blood, sweat, and tubing that the previous owner put into it over the past two years. If you've done this all before and have a hangar full of things like piloted cutters and hole flanging tools, then you're probably too busy to be reading this. Go back out to the hangar where you belong! But if this is your first trip down the altar with an older airplane, use all the smarts you can find. Join clubs; talk to mechanics; go play, look, and talk. Offer to buy gas for a ride—that works for almost anyone.

The more you know about the airplane, the better off you'll be when it comes time to buy.

C-120 and C-140 Rating
Investment: #4
Utility: #5
Popularity: #3

Cessna 170

With post-war prosperity booming along two years after World War II had ended, a lot of businessmen were looking to the air to ensure that their companies would be the first to bring customers all the benefits that they were soon going to realize they

---

C-170 Specifications

Engine: Continental C-145 of 145hp with 1,800-hour TBO
Maximum Weight: 2,200lb
Fuel Capacity: 37.5gal
Maximum Speed: 140mph
Range: 500 miles at 8.0gph
Cruising Speed: 120mph at 5,000ft
Rate of Climb: 690fpm
Service Ceiling: 15,500ft
Landing Speed with Flaps Down, Power Off: 52mph
Empty Weight: 1,200lb
Useful Load: 1,000lb
Wing Span: 36ft
Length: 25ft
Height: 6ft, 7in

needed. Also, something was going to have to be done with all the wartime production capacity that the U. S. aircraft manufacturers had built up since December 1941, when we entered what was soon to be called World War II. Now American enterprise was going to start covering ground using the airplane.

Cessna saw the emerging aircraft market as a chance to bring out an airplane aimed at the person who flew, as well as drove, to the next meeting. The result was the C-170, a true four-place light airplane at what was then a low base price. A new C-170 could be yours for the minor sum of $5,995. For that price you actually got enough parts, pointed in the same direction, to fly. But remember that back in the late forties a new house out of town a ways (they hadn't invented suburbs yet) could be picked up for about the same price. Lifting your body off the earth and propelling it forward through the air isn't cheap now, and it wasn't cheap then.

The C-170 was built, in one guise or another, for nine years. Then somebody at Cessna had the bright idea of relocating the little wheel in the back up front, under the nose. The modified 170 needed a new name, so the 172 was born.

Moving the third wheel to the front made a major difference in the way the airplane handled. It didn't do ground loops any more. Nobody missed those ground loops, so the improvement signaled the demise of the old C-170. If you've ever had the supreme pleasure of watching the runway rotate around the main gear of your airplane, you probably agree that the change was for the best.

A lot of old, experienced pilots will tell you that when the gear was changed to a tricycle type from the conventional taildragger, the romance and talent went out of flying. If you consider riding a 2,200lb trike backwards at 50mph, while trying to steer it in a 12mph crosswind, romance and talent—then I say more power to you. Frankly, the tricycle wins every time, as far as I'm concerned.

As an aside, can you picture a Boeing 747 taildragger? Scary thought.

Anyway, Cessna's idea of the perfect "businessman-pilot's" airplane was first manufactured in March of 1948. The first year C-170s were all metal fuselage with fabric-covered wings. Cessna sold 729 of the C-170s that year.

In 1949, Cessna revamped the 170, building an aluminum wing with a larger fuel capacity of 42gal. The tail was changed a bit, mostly for cosmetic reasons; then the model designation changed to the C-170A. Only a few of the first-year model, with constant-chord fabric wings and two struts, show up for sale each year. Some owners of the 1948 models have recovered their wings in aluminum; some stayed with the fabric, although most of the fabric wings are now done in Ceconite instead of the original cotton cloth. With proper care, the fabric wings should stand up for ten years or longer. A hangar does wonders for making rag-wing airplanes last.

Now, with most of the 170s having been through restoration at least once and headed for collector status, most of what you will find for sale will have had better care than the average 172. Checking around, I located two 1948 C-170s for sale. One was still fabric, while the other had been changed to metal. In both cases the owners were asking about $20,000. Both planes had panels modified with the addition of almost everything but an autopilot: new radios, transponders, loran, and the like. Both were advertised as in totally restored condition. Neither owner was willing to work the price down over the phone. Actually, their responses were more along the lines of, "I know what I've got, what it's worth, and what I'll take. I'm more than willing to keep it until the right money shows up."

Cessna built the C-170A until 1952, when the flaps were improved and the interior changed around a bit. This resulted in the C-170B. Still had the same 145hp motor with fixed-pitch prop, but now it was called the Continental O-300.

Altogether, a few more than 5,100 were built up into 1957, although the factory says production officially ended in 1955. According to Cessna's records, the 170B was still for sale alongside the 172 in 1957, with about 36 being sold that year. So it's possible to find a 1957 C-170 for sale even though it was supposedly dropped when the 172 came along.

The 170 is fairly easy to board, unless the front seats have positive stops installed on the seat rails. The one I looked at had pins through the holes in the seat rails, as per an Airworthiness Directive (AD), so the seat travel stopped before the end of the rail. This is intended to stop the seat from sliding all the way aft, if the locking pin fails to stay in the rail hole. This it does admirably. It also adds a new challenge to climbing around the door while trying to lift into the cockpit. Smaller pilots won't have as much problem with the gymnastics involved. No, I'm not a smaller pilot.

Once inside, visibility over the nose is ok, better than the visibility from a lot of tail-draggers, and the seats are fairly comfortable. The noise level is comparable to other airplanes of that era. Loud! An investment in a good intercom and a pair of high-dollar headsets will go a long way towards saving your hearing. Also, not needing to hold the mike while trying to taxi in a crosswind, when you wish you had at least one more of everything to work the controls, will prove to be a blessing.

Crosswinds, ah yes, crosswinds. And a taildragger that likes to weathervane. If you are coming from something in the 150 or 172 class, be ready for a whole new meaning to the rudder pedals. You can't get by with the sloppy habits you picked up from driving a plane onto the runway like you did with the tricycle-geared airplanes.

Remember, the old adage still holds that you don't quit flying a taildragger until it's tied down.

I'll never forget one pilot who tried to bring his taildragger down a long taxiway back to the hangar but couldn't: when he tried to turn across the intersection, away from the wind, the airplane wanted to go the other way, and won. The pilot had to spin a complete 270 in the opposite direction, around to where he wanted to go, so that he could end up in the spot he wanted to be, instead of where the airplane was trying to go.

Once in the air, the Cessna 170 is a pleasure to fly. It is quite predictable in the stall, without any tendency to drop a wing. A slight release of pressure on the controls and it's flying again.

After adding power at takeoff, the 170 will lift off after about a 750ft roll. Only a light forward pressure on the yoke is required to raise the tail, with the mains coming off the ground at 55mph or so, depending on weight. If you are flying by yourself, expect to see over 900fpm rate of climb. With the 170 at its 2,200lb maximum weight, the rate of climb will drop to the 700fpm range.

The 170 will run 120mph in cruise at 65 percent power and an altitude of 4,500ft. The Continental will burn 8gph at this speed, turning 2,450rpm.

The 170 is stable in all three axes, making for a nice cross-country airplane. It does require coordinated operation between the rudder and yoke to make smooth, synchronized turns. You can't just drive it through the air with your feet firmly planted on the floor. You do have to play stick and rudder in this airplane. But then that's how we all fly, don't we?

Some people consider the C-170 an easy airplane to land, for a taildragger. However, if you carry too much speed on final, it will float nicely down the runway until it runs out of speed and lift. That's when you learn about hop and bounce.

The only way to land the 170, or any light plane for that matter, is in a full-stall attitude. Three pointing it on the runway with the tail-wheel touching just slightly before the mains is the easiest way to land. After you've built some time and learned what the airplane does when it makes the transition from rudder authority to ground handling, you can begin to work with wheeling the airplane on with the tail up, landing on the main gear first, then holding the tail off with forward pressure on the yoke until the speed decays enough for the tailwheel to set down on the runway.

This is a method better learned with a taildragger instructor, rather on your own. You don't absolutely need someone to teach you how to wheel it on, but I have seen it done wrong in the past. And Continental does say that the engine has to be opened up if there is a prop strike. Better to let an expert

A Cessna 180 on short final, flaps down, cowl flaps closed and the spring gear relaxed.

teach you the proper way. That way he can keep you from making too many mistakes. Plus, he's there to save you from the ones that you do make, preventing you from trying to rip out the runway boundary lights like someone I know tried to do with a C-180 a few years back. (But I missed them all.)

So, if your fondest wish is to own a Cessna 170, talk to people who own them, find a good one, get some dual instruction with a taildragger instructor, and then find some small grass strips to play on and enjoy your airplane.

It's a nice, simple plane that, if taken care of, will probably return the full purchase price, or even a little more, when it comes time to sell.

C-170 Rating
Investment: #3
Utility: #4
Popularity: #4

Cessna 180 and 185 Skywagon

Now that you've decided to head on down to Mexico for three or four weeks of flying, fishing, eating shrimp, and getting to know the Tecate Brewing Company a whole lot better, it's time to pick out an airplane.

You don't want one of those strange

ones, with the gear hanging under the engine. You want a real airplane, something that'll get in and out of 1,000ft grass strips when the temperature is above 100 degrees, with a humidity percentage to match.

Oh yeah, you also want to be able to fill all the seats with your friends. (Someone's gotta help with the gas money now that Mexico's devalued the peso. Might as well be people you know.) Then there's the 135lb of Seri Indian ironwood carvings that you bought from the local craftsmen up in Bahia Kino, stuffed under the luggage. And the last suitcase is going to be a little hard to get to at Customs, as it had to be beat into the top of the luggage compartment with a rock that got thrown in along with the rest of the cargo. For the kids at home or something.

What do you mean, heavy? Why, the weight and balance placard must be here someplace. The plane can't be over gross—can it?

Well, if it doesn't get off the ground in the first 500ft, we'll just taxi home up Mexico Highway 15.

Sounds strange? Kinda like whoever thought he's the pilot, needs to talk to an FAA examiner?

You're pretty sure that if the old 172 had that much stuffed inside it, not only would

This is when all you have learned about taildraggers will come into play in the next two seconds.

Contrast the stance of the landing gear to the next picture with the airplane's weight on the ground.

you have to fly it sitting on the strut (because you couldn't get in the pilot's seat), but you'd also set a new world's record for longest taxi without liftoff. You'd need a road map, not a flight chart.

Well, in a slightly scaled-down version of this story, myself and some other people in a group called The Baja Bush Pilots (address in the appendix) have spent a few years traveling down through Mexico sharing one sort of adventure after another.

Always our choice of airplane for short, tight strips has been the Cessna 180 or 185. I wasn't able to afford a 180 on my first couple of trips down into Baja, but after a few years of beating my Cherokee 140 to death, trying to get in and out of strips like Alfonsina's, a hard-packed sand runway partially under water at high tide, I knew it was time for a change.

So the trusty, sorta rusty, 1967 Cherokee had to go. Something better had to be found. Something that would carry a good load, with short, rough field capabilities.

I knew by that time that the only airplane sorta within my price range that could do what I needed was the Cessna 180 or its bigger brother, the 185.

Now, at that time (1984), there were only my wife and I, with no plans for any children, so I went hunting the C-180, a plane I felt would haul most anything that needed to go to Mexico. If I had known that in three years there would be two friends along (one of whom liked to bring home big things), then the 185 would have been the choice. With a load capacity around 1,000lb after the tanks were full, even my souvenir-collecting friend would have been hard put to overload the C-185.

What I opted for was a 1955 C-180. It had the standard Cessna Automatic Radio Corporation (ARC) radio package, a transponder with Mode C, an ADF (automatic direction finder), an intercom, and not much else. It also had the smaller tanks first installed on the 180, so I only had 53gal of usable fuel. It burned 12–13gph. Fuel stops in Baja were sometimes 48gal apart, so range planning became critical. For that reason, you'd be better served with a 180 with the

88gal capacity. However, my checkbook went into nervous prostration when it was time to pay the old owner of 9270 Charlie. The possibility of buying anything newer was slim to none. 70 Charlie it was. Turned out to be one of the smarter things I did in my ten years of Baja flying. That's when I re-

---

C-180 and C-185 Typical Specifications:

Engine, C-180:
1953—Continental O-470-A of 225hp with 1,500-hour TBO
1956—Continental O-470 of 230hp with 1,500-hour TBO
Engine, C-185:
1961—Continental IO-470-F of 260hp with 1,500-hour TBO
1966—Continental IO-520-D of 300hp with 1,700-hour TBO
1985—Continental IO-520-D of 320hp with 1,700-hour TBO
Maximum Weight, 1979 C-180: 2,800lb
Maximum Weight, 1979 C-185: 3,350lb
Fuel Capacity: 88gal
Maximum Speed, C-180: 148kt
Maximum Speed, C-185: 155kt
Maximum Cruise, C-180: 142kt at 75% power and 7,500ft
Maximum Cruise, C-185: 145kt at 75% power and 7,500ft
Range, C-180: 825nm, 5.9 hours with 84gal usable fuel at 8,000ft
Range, C-185: 680nm, 4.7 hours with 84gal usable fuel at 7,500ft
Rate of Climb, C-180: 1,100fpm
Rate of Climb, C-185: 1,010fpm
Service Ceiling, C-180: 17,700ft
Service Ceiling, C-185: 17,150ft
Takeoff Performance, C-180: 625ft ground roll; 1,250ft over 50ft obstacle
Takeoff Performance, C-185: 770ft ground roll; 1,365ft over 50ft obstacle
Landing Performance, C-180: 480ft ground roll; 1,365ft over 50ft obstacle
Landing Performance, C-185: 480ft ground roll; 1,400ft over 50ft obstacle
Stall Speed with Flaps Down, Power Off, C-180: 48kt
Stall Speed with Flaps Down, Power Off, C-185: 49kt
Standard Empty Weight, C-180: 1,643lb
Standard Empty Weight, C-185: 1,681lb
Maximum Useful Load, C-180: 1,167lb
Maximum Useful Load, C-185: 1,681lb
Wing: 35ft, 10in
Length: 25ft, 7.5in
Height: 7ft, 9in

With all the load transferred from the wings to the gear, the wheels assume a straight up, wider stance. The tailwheel is fully steerable.

The 180's bigger brother, the 185. This particular airplane has the optional observation doors and overhead skylights and is swinging a three-bladed prop.

This view shows the overhead skylights on the 185. This airplane looked as though it had rolled off the showroom floor about ten minutes ago. Very nice taildragger.

ally learned how to fly, after seven years of driving tricycle-geared airplanes through the sky. It went a lot of places, and I learned a lot about flying.

Cessna introduced the 180 in 1953 to be a workhorse. Most of the fancy plastic and trick upholstery didn't make the cut for the 180. It's a straightforward, no-frills airplane meant to go to work and earn a living. Back in the seventies, it began to be used extensively on ranches and farms, working out of semi-improved runways or dirt roads.

The one I had purchased didn't have any wheel pants and had been set up with oversized tires for working off dirt. After it taught me how it wanted to be flown, putting it down on a dirt strip was actually easier than on asphalt. I think part of its liking for dirt was that it didn't bounce as much on dirt as it seemed to on paved strips. (My fault? Naw. I always made flawless wheel landings—at least twice in the two years it let me fly it.)

The 180 is an airplane that has to be flown, not driven, through the sky. If you learned to fly in a taildragger, then the C-180 will be a joy to fly. If, like me, all that's in your logbook is tricycle gear stuff, then go find an instructor and be prepared to sweat.

Funny how just sitting in a cockpit, moving a yoke and rudder pedals mere inches, can bring on so much sweat, isn't it? You actually will get over the dry-mouth, wet-palms feeling after a few hours practicing lots of touch-and-go's in the 180. Flying it will turn out to be a ball. Landing will be even more fun.

The flaps are manual, activated by a long lever between the seats. None of those sissy electric switches for the 180, just a long bar to pull.

Having manual flaps gives you the opportunity to play some fairly impressive games in either the 180 or 185. Slow down to 85 or 90mph and crank in full flaps all in one smooth movement. Next point the airplane down at the ground at what seems an impossibly steep angle—the glide angle of a lawn dart. Then the fun begins. First though, you should take the time to become acquainted with the trim wheel, because you'll be wearing the finish off it in short order. That's if it has any finish whatsoever left. Probably it's been spun so much that the knobs around the edge have been rounded off to the point that the wheel is one smooth circle.

Anyway, there you sit at 85mph, with the spinner pointed at the numbers on the runway, the trim all set so you don't have to hold the yoke forward. Now what?

Well, after some practice playing helicopter, you'll find that the 180 will simply head for the earth at 800fpm or so, with no climb in airspeed. Then, before it goes thud, say 100ft above ground level (AGL), you bring the yoke back, trim the ship to a slight-

Some of the older taildraggers show a bit of wear. This airbox has obviously seen the attentions of a rivet gun more than once. With parts scarce to nonexistent, the old stuff has to be used. Sometimes it's repair the older repair on the first repair.

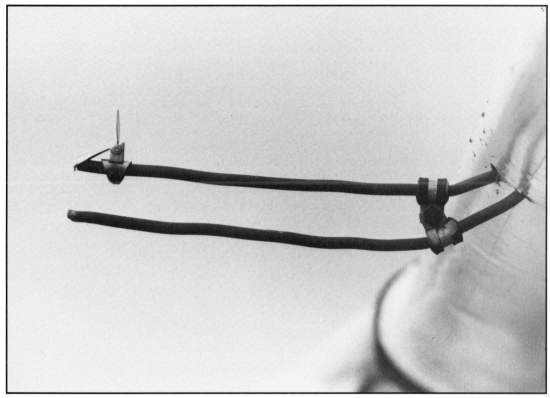

A "slightly modified" pitot tube and air speed sensor. Beware of airplanes with such obviously crude modifications.

ly nose-high attitude, and fly to a normal, full-stall landing. This is why it's critical to get a good taildragger instructor, someone who can teach you how to really fly the 180. Making a mistake at this point could interfere with your future logbook entries.

The bush pilots, those who make their living doing what we think we'd like to do, use the short-field capabilities of the 180 series to get into strips that you and I would classify as driveways—real short driveways. Given the slightest excuse for an airstrip, the 180 will set down and stop before most airplanes have figured out that the mains are on the ground. As I said above, the C-180 seems to prefer flying out of places that any self-respecting seagull would give a pass.

The C-185, introduced in 1961, is a 180 with all the benefits of more horsepower, higher gross, and a small increase in empty weight. The later C-185s are fitted with the Continental IO-520D engine, rated at 300 strong ponies. It has the same airframe as the C-180. The two look quite similar on the outside, especially when each is seen alone. Both are taildraggers, both have straight tails.

Things change though, under the aluminum. The framework is much different in the 185, with more bracing and a totally new, stronger wing to carry 500-plus additional pounds of useful load. And if seen together, the 180 and 185 are actually quite easy to tell apart. The 180 has only one window behind the door, while the C-185 has two. And the 185's larger cabin is quite identifiable with both airplanes side-by-side.

The 185 is also called the Skywagon, and in this case, the plane deserves its name. It

A new 1962 Cessna 180 going ranching. *Cessna Aircraft Company*

Cessna's promo picture of a C-180 for 1963. Wonder what's in all those cardboard boxes on the tailgate of the new for 1963 Ford station wagon? *Cessna Aircraft Company*

has room for six real people with enough room left over to carry all their luggage. (As long as they keep the rocks and ironwood down to a reasonable load.) It will take a 1,600lb load at 160mph for a 600-mile trip to a 1,000ft dirt strip. Plus, when the pilot knows his job, the 185 will work out of that same tight airstrip as though it were Los Angeles International.

One of the challenges of flying to Mexico with the Baja Bush Pilots was the contest of getting in and out of a 1,200ft strip. It was set up for people who thought a 4,000ft runway was tight going. Everybody who played the game had to really plan what, where, and how the airplane was going to perform.

Arnold Senterfitt, the man responsible for the Baja Bush Pilots, and the author of the definitive book on travels through Mexico and Central America, set up a competition among members to see if they could take whatever airplane they were flying, be it Bonanza or Cessna or anything in between, and work it out of a 1,200ft runway on one of the airstrips in Mexico. He set up the contest course on the runway at Santa Ynez, a paved runway 200nm south of Mexicali. Then he would stand back and see who could take off and return to land within the given length.

He had various ratings for pilots who could get their airplanes in and out of the measured distance without running over the mark. More a measure of skill than a contest. A good way to teach pilots the capability of their airplanes when skill ruled the day.

I was flying a rented 1979 Mooney 201 at the time, just having parted with a Cherokee 140. Even with the help of a very talented Bo-

Even the pilot wears a tie (and a bow tie at that) in this brand-new C-185 Skywagon. Wheel pants were not often installed on the taildraggers as original equipment. *Cessna Aircraft Company*

A Cessna 185 up on floats at a sport show in 1963. The advertising department worked overtime to come up with catchy slogans for their airplanes and environs. "Utililand" indeed! Slogans aside, I'd give quite a bit to own this amphibious 185. *Cessna Aircraft Company*

nanza pilot who spent most of his working life in the left seat of a United Airlines 747, I always seemed to end up at the 1,250ft mark on landing with a great deal of screeching of tires, scorching of brake pads, and scratching of head.

What really made me put on my hair shirt, replete with whimpering and sniveling, was, after all the "new guys," including me, were finished making black marks on the runway, Arnold would load up his 185 with people, luggage, lunches, and his everpresent measuring wheel, crank up the engine, taxi out onto the runway, and make us all look silly by picking up the tail in less than 300ft, the rest of the airplane leaving the ground after a 700ft roll. Talk about humbling.

No one yet has figured out how to go back in time. If it ever became possible, my hours in the C-180 would be the first place I would go. Picture landing on Isla Natividad on a Saturday morning. It's a watchstrap-thin piece of dirt and rocks fourteen miles off the coast of Baja. The people on the island use fresh lobster (less than two hours old) to pay for a ride to the mainland. The runway is adjacent to the only restaurant on the island, so we taxied up and parked in the shade of the only tall tree on the island and walked about a hundred feet to a lunch of broiled lobster, shrimp, and tortillas. Not quite like blowing from one indistinguishable airport to another, filling one more two-point, three-hour cross-country into the ol' logbook. I'd go back in a second.

The point is that a 180 or 185 is probably the most capable airplane, next to a Helio Courier, to take a group of people (up to six) away from civilization to airports and adventures that could only be dreamed about in most airplanes.

If you have spent all your flying career landing on nice, well-lighted, paved runways, you owe it to yourself to go find out what flying is really like when the pavement turns to grass and the airplane is a Cessna 180 taildragger.

Oh, and call me if you want a copilot. I'll buy the gas!

C-180 and C-185 Rating
Investment: #1
Utility: #1
Popularity: #3

Chapter 3

The Ubiquitous

Cessna 150 and 152

There may be a few pilots out there who haven't flown a Cessna 150 or 152, but most of their licenses are probably dated back when airplanes had wooden wheels. A majority of us have had the pleasure of spending a few hours in that airplane's cabin, trying to remember what's the next checkpoint and why're the hands so sweaty. A lot of us spent our first few minutes alone in a flying airplane in one of these two trainers.

Cessna had been out of the two-seat aircraft business since the last C-140 rolled out the door in 1950. They determined that the market was ready for a new trainer. The new airplane was to be called the 150, following Cessna's practice of using numbers in the century series.

The 150 was fitted with the 172's tricycle landing gear and given a Continental engine rated at 100hp—ten more than the engine in the Cessna 140. This horsepower increase really didn't give the 150 a great deal more performance over the older 140. The extra go just let everything happen a little easier with some additional comfort thrown in for good measure. Sort of a scaled down 172 with quicker response.

Back in the late sixties, around seven million flight-training hours were flown in this country. Of that number a little over three million were flown in the Cessna 150. The airplanes were grabbed as fast as they came off the assembly line and sent out in the world to start generating money for flight schools and to grow a crop of new pilots in the process.

They were touted in the same vein as their bigger brother as "drive 'em on, drive 'em off" types of airplanes. Cessna even used the term "Land-o-Matic" when describing the new tricycle-geared airplanes. What I want to know is, if they were so easy to drive onto the runway, why did the one that I was flying at the time seem to want to bounce so much when I tried to plant it on the asphalt? Must

"Now, let's try not to bounce it again on this landing." Another student sweats out a lesson.

have been overinflated tires or something. Sure squealed a lot, too, when the brakes went on—wonder if they were rusty or old. Couldn't have been me, could it?

I guess if I could obtain my private pilot's certificate without destroying one of Mr. Cessna's airplanes, they must have been put together fairly stoutly at the factory.

True story. The Cessna in which I learned to fly was involved in a "I didn't see 'em" type of midair collision a year after I got my ticket, about five miles out on a long final to the runway. Both airplanes went down, the Cessna without part of a wing and with no windshield. I didn't hear what happened to the other airplane, a low wing single, but the one that I had been using as a trainer landed safely in a grassy field. The owner of the FBO and his chief mechanic went out to look it over that afternoon. The A&P mechanic figured that with a windshield and some minor work (lots of speed tape), the airplane could be flown back to base. So while the owner tapdanced with the FAA about getting a ferry permit, the mechanic installed a new windscreen, straightened some sheet metal, and hung about five hundred yards of silver tape on the wing. Next morning, real early, the chief pilot for the club (he was the smallest) performed a very careful preflight, lit off the engine, pointed the 152 down a dirt path, and hopped the five miles back to the airport uneventfully—very carefully.

Nothing major was bent on the Cessna, so it was mostly a case of replacing sheet metal, reriveting panels, and replacing a few unrepairable parts; and the airplane was signed off safe to fly.

I had enough faith in Cessna's quality and the repair work performed by the FBO that I was the first to take it around the patch after the repairs. 'Course, I'm real brave and a fearless pilot—didn't even sweat at all.

Weeell, maybe just a little.

The real reason I flew it was that I was in the process of buying the airplane when the accident occurred. I had an interest in seeing that it flew straight. As it worked out, the airplane was OK. It stayed with me for three years, mostly teaching students and occasion-

---

C-150 and C-152 Typical Specifications:

Engine:
1959 C-150—Continental O-200-A of 100hp with 1,800-hour TBO
1978 C-152—Lycoming O-235-L2C of 110hp with 2,400-hour TBO
Maximum Weight:
1959 C-150—1,500lb
1964 C-150—1,600lb
1978 C-152—1,670lb
1978 Aerobat—1,670lb
Fuel Capacity: 26gal
Maximum Cruise Speed, 1976 C-150: 106kt at 75% power and 7,000ft
Maximum Cruise Speed, 1978 C-152: 107kt at 75% power and 8,000ft
Range: 340nm, 3.5 hours with 22.5gal usable fuel at 7,000ft, C-150
Range: 350nm, 3.4 hours with 24.5gal usable fuel, C-152
Rate of Climb, C-150: 670fpm
Rate of Climb, C-152: 715fpm
Service Ceiling, C-150: 14,000ft
Service Ceiling, C-152: 14,700ft
Takeoff Performance, C-150: 735ft ground roll; 1,385ft over 50ft obstacle
Takeoff Performance, C-152: 725ft ground roll; 1,340ft over 50ft obstacle
Landing Performance, C-150: 445ft ground roll; 1,075ft over 50ft obstacle
Landing Performance, C-152: 475ft ground roll; 1,200ft over 50ft obstacle
Stall Speed with Flaps Up, Power Off, C-150: 46kt
Stall Speed with Flaps Up, Power Off, C-152: 48kt
Stall Speed with Flaps Down, Power Off, C-150: 42kt
Stall Speed with Flaps Down, Power Off, C-152: 43kt
Maximum Weight, C-150: 1,600lb
Maximum Weight, C-152: 1,670lb
Standard Empty Weight, C-150: 1,104lb
Standard Empty Weight, C-152: 1,081lb
Maximum Useful Load, C-150: 496lb
Maximum Useful Load, C-152: 589lb
Wing Span: 33ft, 2in
Length, C-150: 23ft, 11in
Length, C-152: 24ft, 1in
Height: 8ft, 6in

---

ally taking me and a friend out for a quick lunch hop.

Each year of production, Cessna incorporated various changes into the 150. Some of the modifications were nothing more than cosmetics to enable a person to differentiate between the model years. Some, however, were major. The first big one was in 1959 when the TBO on the Continental engine went from 600 hours to 1,800 hours. In effect, Continental tripled the life of the engine. A rather major change.

In 1961 the main gear was pushed back two inches to put more weight on the nose wheel, eliminating the light nose feeling of the earlier models. The same year saw adjustable seats for the first time. No more pillows in the luggage space for different-sized students.

Larger tires (6.00 x 6) came along in 1963 along with quick-drain fuel strainers.

In 1964 the appearance of the 150 changed with the introduction of Cessna's "Omni-Vision," adding rear windows to the fuselage.

In 1967 the company built the 150 with Omni-Vision and a swept tail, setting the look for all the 150s and 152s to come.

Like most other Cessnas, the 150 picked up some weight as the years went by. Customers were willing to lose a little payload as

If you really didn't know what model of airplane this is, Cessna was kind enough to write 152 on the tail in large letters. The student pilot is practicing full stop landings, staying in the pattern for an hour or

so. Hard work in a small cockpit, especially when the runway temperature is over 90 degrees. His window is closed, he just called the tower to taxi out for one more takeoff.

Look closely, you can see the step on the landing gear and on the strut of this 152. This makes checking the fuel tanks in the wings easier for the student. The door shows that it has seen its fair share of students. Since Cessna no longer builds trainers, the ones still in service are racking up a lot of hours. This 152 has 6,300hr on the airframe.

a tradeoff for a more comfortable airplane or more avionics. After all, with a base price of $6,995 for the standard model in 1958, one couldn't expect too many frills or very much in the panel.

As a point of comparison, in *Trade-A-Plane*, second March issue 1993, there is a fairly nice 1959 going for $10,900 with 3,557 TT, 487 Since Major Overhaul (SMOH) and one ARC radio. In the same issue a loaded 1983 Model 152 is being offered for the measly sum of $29,900. Who'da thunk in 1958 that the 150 and its successor would have sold for the price of an apartment building. And from what the flight schools say, the airplane won't get any cheaper.

In 1970, Cessna brought out the Model A-150 Aerobat. It was a 150 with structural strengthening to allow it to pull up to 6 Gs positive and 3 Gs negative load. Cessna intended it to be an airplane in which a pilot could strap on a parachute, fasten the quick-release harnesses, take it up and go fly barrel rolls, snap rolls, aileron rolls, spins, chandelles, and other aerobatic maneuvers.

The International Aerobatic Club (IAC) contestants aren't going to lose any sleep worrying about the Cessna Aerobat blowing their Sukhois or Extra 200s out of the sky. But an average pilot can buy an Aerobat, line up an aerobatics instructor, get some hours in unusual attitudes (like upside down), and generally amuse himself to no end.

The Aerobat also serves a good purpose for the general pilot who isn't real fond of spins and loops but who wants to learn more about what an airplane does when it's not straight and level. After all, these things do operate in three dimensions. It's entirely possible that one could encounter severe turbulence sometime during a flying career. Wouldn't it be nice to have a few akro hours logged when the airplane decides that it would really like to fly all kinds of sideways no matter what you want? Knowing how to react to an unusual attitude or flying condition, when the airplane is pointed in a direction that you'd prefer not to go, can be very useful.

Also flying upside down can be fun . . . really.

On a nice sunny day, playing around with loops and rolls in a 150 Aerobat can be an excellent way to work the kinks out of a grinding week. Plus, making the world revolve around your windscreen while going through an aileron roll will definitely take your mind off what the boss said to you last Thursday. Great fun!

In April 1977, Cessna began delivering what would be its last two-seat airplane, the Model 152. Although it was delivered in 1977, it was considered a 1978 model.

The single biggest change from the 150 was the move to Lycoming for the powerplant. The new engine was a four-cylinder 235ci rated at 110hp. The idea behind the different motor was to have an engine that would handle the reduced lead content of the new 100 Low Lead (LL) gasoline that replaced the 80 and 100-130 octane aviation fuels that were rapidly disappearing from the fuel farms.

Also, the new 152 had a 28-volt electrical system, replacing the older, weaker 12-volt system in the 150. One drawback to the revised electrics is that if you leave the master on overnight, you can't use your car battery to light off the 152. You have to go over to your local FBO and let them know you did a dumb thing.

Don't worry; you won't be the first.

I left the master switch on after a long, tiring, cross-country flight to San Felipe Airport in Baja California. There are absolutely no services available in San Felipe. Except for an occasional airport attendant and the ever-present uniformed guard, we had the airport to ourselves. So we had to hand prop the engine to get going.

A point to consider about the 152. It has an alternator for a charging system, as do most other post-1975 airplanes. This means that if you have to hand prop the engine to start it, the alternator won't work. A power source is required to the field coils to start the alternator charging. So, unless your aircraft is equipped with an alternator restart switch, as in the Cessna O-2A (the military version of the Model 337 Skymaster), all you will have is a running engine. You won't have any radios, lorans, navs, lights, or anything else that draws electrical power.

Speaks volumes for carrying a handheld radio as a backup.

Yes, I do have one; yes, we had it that day; and boy, did it make me feel better on the way to Mexicali Airport at the border. We were able to get a quick charge at Mexicali while we went through customs and filed our one-hour notice with the San Diego Flight Service Station (FSS). Everything worked as advertised with the battery up to snuff. The rest of the trip went quite uneventfully. I guess I only get to do one major dumb per trip.

Total Model 150 production in the US was 22,082. The 150s were also made under license at Reims, France. The number produced there was 1,758. The Model 152 was built from 1977 to 1984 with a total of 6,747 built in the US. An additional 573 were built in Reims. All in all, this plane was the most popular trainer ever built.

C-150 and C-152 Rating
Investment: #1
Utility: #1
Popularity: #1

Cessna 172 Skyhawk

The title of this chapter is "The Ubiquitous," which means "widespread." The Cessna 172 and its ilk are nothing if not widespread. At last count, the 172 accounted for just about ten percent of the general-aviation airplanes. The 172 was first introduced in 1956.

It would be simple to just say "How much you got is how much you get" when contemplating a Cessna 172 purchase, although that's simplifying matters a lot. Actually, there is quite a bit more to buying a 172 than simply throwing money at it until it's yours.

An awful lot of would-be pilots spent their first sweaty-handed hour in a 172, of one flavor or another, on the long road to private pilot. Usually this ensures that any 172 you look at with over 3,000 hours on the tach probably spent most of its time going around the patch as a trainer. Not that this is necessarily bad, you understand, but trainers seem to take a higher amount of abuse than privately flown craft.

As an example, one of our school planes,

A 172 about to touch down. Full flaps and the power at idle.

Another 172 on the runway, taking off. The front tire looks a tad low.

with 4,570 hours on the clock, has spent most of its life as a trainer at San Jose's Reid-Hillview Airport, where most of the operation is on Runway 31R with all the resultant turnoffs to the right to Taxiway 2. Every turn is to the right. Two weeks ago, as N18BB came up for one of its 100 hours inspections, I had a chance to look at its logbook to see what had been falling off with what regularity.

Interesting. Very interesting.

Turns out that the shop is replacing the right brake pad approximately every 25 hours. However, the left one has been on the airplane so long that the backing plate is rusting away.

Think the students are dragging the right brake around the taxiway a little?

So, being of a suspicious mind, I pulled the logs for the club's Cessna 182, an airplane not used for primary training. As a matter of fact, the 182 had spent the last 230 hours in long cross-country flights, with one long, 17 hours roundtrip to Baja California's Cabo San Lucas, about 1,600nm from home base. (Yes,

This is what most people envision when they hear "small airplane." A nice Skyhawk II taxis out.

the water's warm and the shrimp's fresh.)

No surprises here. The logs showed that the brakes were "fully serviceable" as of the last 100 hours inspection, two months ago. Both brake pads showed little wear.

This little vignette is put forth not to show that new students have a tendency to ride the brakes while rolling down the runway or turning for a taxi-back. I mean, I didn't when I was learning. Did you? It's just a way of illustrating how a trainer spends its life and wears out its parts.

Parts . . . yes, parts. Like the $37.50 landing light bulb that goes south every 40 hours or so of operation. Students are now being encouraged to keep on the landing light while in the air, and the filaments in the bulb

get quite hot after being on for over an hour. Then, when the instructor suggests while on short final, "Let's make this one a short-field approach, then practice a few touch-and-gos," you can picture what kind of pounding the bulb is going to get while sweaty hands are trying to plant the 172 on the first 50ft of the runway. Sometimes, it seems, students try to land about 4ft under the runway, with the usual controlled-crash arrival and bounce, as the 172 gets forced on the runway a lot harder than it wanted to be. Occasionally it gets to land three or four times for every trip down the runway.

I wonder, do the students log each bounce as a landing, no matter how short a time the airplane stays on the ground?

Aftermarket drooped wing tips on an older C-172. These wing tips were advertised to decrease take-off distance and increase both cruise speed and climb rate. Some say they add a lot; others disagree. They do change the looks of the airplane, though. This 172 has no wheel pants, and probably has seen a few dirt strips in its time.

C-172 Typical Specifications

Engine:
1956—Continental O-300-A of 145hp
1960—Continental O-300-C of 145hp
1962—Continental O-300-D of 145hp
1968—Lycoming O-320-E2D of 150hp
1977—Lycoming O-320-H2AD of 150hp (the problem engine)
1981—Lycoming O-320-D2J of 150hp
Maximum Weight:
1956 C-172: 2,200lb
1962 C-172C: 2,250lb
1963 C-172D: 2,300lb
1968 C-172I: 2,300lb
1977 C-172N: 2,300lb
1981 C-172P: 2,400lb
Fuel Capacity: 39–43gal
Maximum Cruise Speed: 125kt at sea level
Range: 485nm, 4.1 hours with 40gal usable fuel at 8,000ft
Range: 630nm, 5.3 hours with 50gal usable fuel at 8,000ft
Rate of Climb: 770fpm at sea level
Service Ceiling: 14,200ft
Takeoff Performance: 805ft ground roll; 1,440ft over 50ft obstacle
Landing Performance: 520ft ground roll; 1,250ft over 50ft obstacle
Stall Speed with Flaps Up, Power Off: 50kt
Stall Speed with Flaps Down, Power Off: 44kt
Standard Empty Weight: 1,393lb
Maximum Useful Load: 907lb
Wing Span: 35ft, 10in
Length: 26ft, 11in
Height: 8ft, 9.5in

The point is that if you're considering purchasing a 172 that has always been a trainer, you want to be very careful when it comes time for a prepurchase inspection. Also, read the log books carefully. Not that a 172 trainer can't be in good condition. It's just that as a trainer it has lived a harder life than a creampuff that's still on the first engine and has less than 2,000 hours on the clock.

On the other hand, letting an airplane sit on the ramp for a lot of years is a good way to ruin it. As you've probably heard from other sources, airplanes are meant to fly, not sit.

In illustration, we purchased a 1971 C-172 that had spent most of its life tied down at Corning Airport, a small 2,700ft runway up in northern California. Well, it showed pretty good for an airplane of its vintage: no oil leaks under the cowl, no corrosion visible, no obvious parts missing. It looked like a fairly good ship in light of what the owners were asking for a purchase price.

Off we go! Four people leaving for the day. The shadow on the runway indicates a late morning departure.

We flew it around a while, then checked the belly for new oil stains and the hydraulics for any appreciable leakage. So far, so good. Even the seat rail holes were round instead of oval. (More on that later.)

What we neglected to do was to pull the plugs to check the cylinder bores with a borescope. Our mistake. Turns out that after 30 hours of flying, the engine was using over one quart of oil per hour. Not good. All the cylinders had to be pulled and rebuilt.

Now, I don't know what a machine shop charges to pull, rebuild, and reinstall a set of cylinders and pistons around your area, but we ended up paying just under $1,000 per

hole. The total bill, with parts, used up most of a $5,000 bill.

Near as can be determined, the airplane sat outside long enough without the engine being turned over or run up that the piston rings rusted onto the cylinder bores. When the previous owners decided to sell, they pulled the prop through a few times to unstick the rings, flew it a while, then changed the oil and cleaned the screens. So when we got to the logs, they showed a fresh oil change and 6 hours of flying in the last few months. Our fault. We should have taken the 172 over to an FBO (different from the one the previous owner was using), had a me-

Once a year comes the annual inspection. Usually it starts with the removal of the engine covers as this is where most of the work will happen.

A close-up of a 172's Continental six-cylinder. The tubing below the engine leads from an intake in front of the engine, over the muffler and into the cockpit for the heater. Behind and below the tubular muffler is the carburetor air intake.

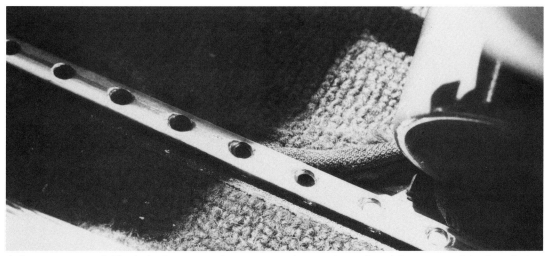

A Cessna's seat rail. The holes have a tendency to elongate with use. At a certain diameter, the rails have to be replaced. In some models, the rails can run up to $800. Check closely before purchase.

This 172's panel has been updated considerably. It has two King KX-170 radios, a Northstar Loran, an audio panel, and older ADF and transponder. This plane's all set to go IFR.

chanic pull the plugs to check the cylinder walls, and then run a compression check. What we would have seen would have been long gouges running down the cylinder walls from where pieces of the broken rings were dragging. We would have known that the engine would have to come apart real soon for major work. Thus, if we had still had an interest in the airplane, the price would have had to have taken a serious drop.

This should be a standard prepurchase inspection for any airplane, because all engines will rust if not exercised regularly.

This time we learn; next time we check.

Earlier, seat rails were mentioned. Lawyers extracted $25 million from Cessna in a case in which seat pins in a Cessna failed to hold in the holes in the floor rails. I wasn't at the trial, and I wasn't in the airplane in question, so bear in mind that anything I say is just opinion.

As the story was reported, a seat in an older Cessna failed to stay latched on takeoff and slid to its full-aft travel. The person flying the airplane held onto the yoke as he and the seat slipped to the rear. The nose pitched

Tow bar, oil bottles, portable step, and torn interior—a well-used 172.

up, and the airplane stalled and crashed. The pilot died in the crash.

The problem turned out to be the holes in the seat rails. They had become elongated from use to the point that any sudden pressure would cause the locating pin on the seat to slip out. As I said above, this is only my opinion, but wouldn't seat rails be part of a preflight inspection in which the pilot is to insure that all aspects of the airplane are checked and the aircraft is safe to fly? Not that Cessna didn't have some level of responsibility in this incident, as was subsequently proven in court. However, all I got out of the matter was that someone died because parts had worn out, and the same someone's attorney was later photographed standing next to a new jet warbird he bought with proceeds from the case.

Again, it's only my opinion, but that case is probably one of the reasons you and I can no longer buy a new Cessna 172, regardless of the cost.

Speaking of cost, just how much will you have to pay for a 172? With the general aviation fleet getting to be twenty-five years old on average, condition will have quite a bearing on price. Last year (1992) a total of 510 single-engine piston airplanes were manufactured—none by Cessna. So if you are going to find a Cessna 172 in new or like-new condition, the probability is high that it will cost at least what it sold for new or up to twenty percent over original factory price.

In another *Trade-A-Plane* ad, the owner of a 1981 Skyhawk with 4,185 TT, 60 hours on a certified chrome engine, new King radios, all the other good stuff in the panel, and a

Over she goes! This 172 has seen lots of care.
The underbelly shows no oil streaks—rare.

Looking through the pilot's door at the back seat in a 172. This shot shows some of the famous Cessna plastic trim. If you look closely at the rear bulkhead it shows some of the famous Cessna plastic trim cracks. Watch out for these small items because the trim isn't cheap.

new interior is asking $52,000. A 1984 with no total time shown, but with 930 hours since overhaul, with the usual radios and other panel equipment, is priced at $55,000.

When you read down at the level I can afford, there is a 1970 with 2,028 TT and only 420 since overhaul, with Cessna/ARC radios, for $21,000 asking.

Cessna 172 prices run the gamut from $15,000 for a 1956 all the way up to $70,000 for one of the last ones manufactured in 1986. All I can say is, that for 70 large, it had better look like it just came out of the box. Lot of money for a 172, but I'm willing to bet it won't get any cheaper with age. If you hang onto whatever you buy, take relatively good care of it, and keep the rubber side down, you'll return a profit when it comes time to sell.

Here are a few of the main problems to watch for when checking over a 172.

Corrosion. Cessna built most of the 172s without any corrosion-proofing inside the airframe, so be sure to check closely. Get a flashlight and a mirror. Look into the places that usually get skipped during annuals.

Look for cracks in the airframe, especially if it was a trainer with high time and lots of landings. Inspect around the landing gear saddle for stress cracks. Look over the tailfeathers closely. Chasing cracks can get to be a very money-draining, time-consuming procedure.

Most importantly, check the engine time. Check not only when the engine was rebuilt, but also who did the work. There is a major difference in value depending on whether the engine was remanufactured to zero time on

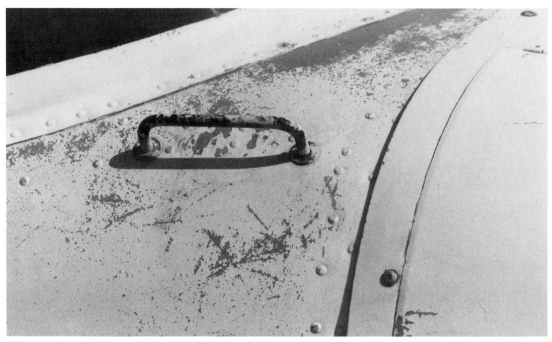

This grab handle has seen a lot of hands, the paint a lot of sun. If you want it to last and retain its value, take care of your airplane.

all its components by the factory or whether it was rebuilt in a hangar by a fence company that does engines when times get slack.

Also, one final word. If the logbooks look as though they went through a course of creative journalism, if the entries start in 1990 for a 1975 Cessna 172, or if the entries are just not there altogether, give the deal a pass. Too many chances for too many interesting (read: expensive!) problems to be hidden in the paperwork.

C-172 Rating
Investment: #1
Utility: #2
Popularity: #1A (Everybody likes the 172)

Cessna 175 Skylark

When Cessna built the C-172 in 1956, no one could have foreseen how far the company would take the airplane twenty years later. Or that it would still be around in twen-

ty years. Cessna managed to cover a lot of options with the same basic airframe. A number of other airplanes were spun off of the same type certificate.

In 1958, the 175 Skylark came along. The idea was to add some more performance using as much of the original 172 as possible while keeping engineering costs down to a dull roar. To make things more interesting in the quest for speed, a geared version of the 172's 145hp motor, rated at 175hp at 3,200rpm, was installed along with a constant-speed prop. What you got was a 30hp bump by spinning the engine a group faster, then gearing down the prop to 2,400rpm to stay within its useful range. What you also got was an engine that was spinning a lot more parts a lot faster. The initial motor in the 172 was happy running around 2,600rpm. Continental took that motor and spun it 600rpm faster to make higher rated horsepower. Probably didn't do much for reliabili-

A sparkling new 1963 Skyhawk. *Cessna Aircraft Company*

ty. I guarantee you, it didn't do anything towards lower operating costs.

Cessna must have thought pilots wanted more complexity with higher maintenance costs at the same time.

Continental threw in a shorter TBO on the engine, mostly due to the greater strain on the moving parts. Plus, if not watched carefully, the gear drive on the engine has a bad habit of developing a lot of slop, which will eventually beat the engine to pieces, if not caught and replaced in time. The engine has to come apart every 1,200 hours, as opposed to a 2,000-hour TBO on the non-geared engine.

Other than that, what you had was a 172 with a little more go and lots more things to play with in the cockpit.

The panel had the usual controls found in any old 172, with a prop control and cowl

---

C-175 Specifications

Engine, 1958: Continental GO-300-E of 175hp with 1,200-hour TBO

Maximum Weight, 1958: 2,350lb

Maximum Weight, 1963: 2,500lb

Fuel Capacity: 52gal

Maximum Cruise: 140mph at 75% power

Range: 585mi

Rate of Climb: 850fpm

Service Ceiling: 17,800ft

Takeoff Performance: 640ft ground roll; 1,340ft to clear 50ft obstacle

Landing Performance: 600ft ground roll; 1,155ft to clear 50ft obstacle

Stall Speed with Flaps Down, Power Off: 50mph

Useful Load:

1958—945lb

1963—1,140lb

Wing Span: 36ft, 2in

Length: 25ft

Height: 8ft, 6in

A fresh and shiny C-172. *Cessna Aircraft Company*

Fourteen Echo loads up with the family from the new 1963 Ford. Looks like four adults and one child are going to jump aboard. Might check the weight and balance. *Cessna Aircraft Company*

If your desires run to an early sixties 172, this is what you want it to look like. *Cessna Aircraft Company*

flap lever added as an extra bonus.

The 175 originally sold for $3,000 more than the similarly equipped 172. The gains in performance were minimal, not really enough to offset the higher operating cost. An engine rebuild for the geared Continental GO-300 will set you back about $9,000–$11,000, unless the drive gear has gone south. Then figure on another $2,000 for parts. The gear on the engine drives a gear on the prop, so usually both have to be replaced.

Most of this shows in the Blue Book. Average retail for a 1963 C-175 is $16,900, while the comparable 172 runs $3,000 higher. Just the reverse of the original selling prices.

If you get the idea that I don't hold a warm spot in my heart for the 175, you could

be right. Cessna didn't either. Production ran from 1958 to 1963, but sales dropped by 1961. The airplane is a lot more maintenance for little, if any, significant gain in speed over a 172.

If you're into cheap and trying to get in the air by springing for an older Cessna, I'd give this airplane a pass. Save money for a while longer, or buy a nice C-150 of the same vintage at the same price.

Probably the biggest reason for my lack of affection for the 175 goes back a few years to an engine rebuild that a neighbor in the adjoining hangar was sweating through on his C-175. To keep the horror story short and not offend widows and orphans, let's just say that after spending large dollars to get the

Continental back together and running, he showed me a totally different side of his personality when the gear between the prop and the engine shattered after a whole 120 hours of operation. He got to do it all over again. All I heard from the other hangar for the next six months were growls and strange mutterings.

Now, I realize this could happen to any airplane, any part. However, when the cost of a rebuild can run 80 percent of the airplane's worth, why set yourself up for more complications. Plus, the engine in just about every airplane flying today has a longer TBO than the 175's engine.

C-175 Rating
Investment: #5
Utility: #5
Popularity: #5

Cessna 172 Hawk XP

Then there is the Hawk XP, or Extra Performance, a hot rod 172.

Cessna did for us what a lot of people talked about doing. Taking a standard C-172 Airframe, pulling its Lycoming O-320 rated at 150hp, Cessna went the "more horsepower, more go" route by installing a Continental IO-360 pumping out 195 ponies. Just to help fill out the model line with a different 172, Cessna also threw in a constant-speed prop, with the idea that some more climb performance could be picked up without losing too much cruise.

Granted, dropping the Continental 195hp injected 360ci engine into the C-172 airframe didn't make the guys at the Sukhoi Design Bureau start looking over their shoulders, wondering if the C-172 XP was going to give their Su-27 a hard time in Air Combat Maneuvers (ACM). But Cessna was trying to build a little more basic airplane, not the next generation Air Superiority Interceptor.

And it seems it succeeded admirably. By all accounts, the XP gained a shorter takeoff roll, about 5kt in cruise and another 250lb in gross weight. It also picked up almost 150lb in empty weight to go along with the increased gross, so the useful load really didn't go up by all that much.

Throw in a few more avionics and other goodies, and the airplane begins to be less for more. The increased weight in the panel takes away some of the 35hp advantage over the standard 172.

The first 1977 model, with the early Continental, only had a 1,500-hour TBO. Subsequent models went to a 2,000-hour TBO, still rated at the same power.

The airplane flies like any low-pop 172 with a few extras added. The trouble is, some of those extras are problems. For example, don't lean the engine to less than 10gph unless you have an undying desire to see what the inside of warped cylinders looks like. Some of the early books stated that the XP could be flown with the engine pulled back to 8gph. This was touted as a great economy feature. The problems didn't start to show until the airplane had been flown at that mixture setting for a few hundred hours, long after all the demo airplanes had gone on to other homes. Then oil consumption and power-loss problems began to appear.

When you go for a demo ride with the owner, watch how he leans the engine above 3,000ft. Whatever he does with you in the airplane, you can be sure that he's been doing the same for many a year. Check it carefully.

You don't have to go to the effort of pulling a cylinder and running a micrometer through it, but a trip through the spark plug holes with a bore scope is definitely indicated on any prepurchase inspection. Especially if you have reason to suspect the previous owner was trying to go cheap on the fuel.

The 172 XPs differ slightly from serial number to serial number, and you may notice the variations, depending on which serial number you end up putting on your insurance policy. The biggest difference is a change in maneuvering speed of certain serial numbers from 105kt to 104kt.

OK, OK, maybe it's no big deal, but Cessna thought so, or it wouldn't have made the change. Probably not something to keep anyone awake nights, but you know how aviation runs. Change the flap extension speed or color of the curtains and, whoopee, a new model.

De-bugging a rare Hawk XP II. This aircraft consisted of a 172 fuselage with a Continental 195hp engine. If you are looking, this is what you want to find, a well-kept, low-time airplane in the $40,000 range. (No, he won't sell or it would be me cleaning bugs off the wing.)

Plus, the XP wasn't built long enough to really get into a lot of changes. It only rolled out of the factory from 1978 to 1981. Hardly enough time for the lawyers to figure out how to spell Hawk XP in a lawsuit.

If a Hawk XP lets you take it home for a while, what kind of performance gains can you expect to see over the plain brown wrapper 172?

Several owners told me what they thought of their version of the XP. Everybody had a different story, but all three were happy with what they had.

All of them agreed that you can expect a speed increase of 5–7kt, at most, over the 172.

Maintenance costs due to the constant-speed prop didn't amount to a great deal, unless the control cable let go in flight (it happened! and livened up the show considerably). This turned out to be a people problem, not an airplane problem. The parts were put together wrong, and they broke.

As an aside, one fact comes to mind. Regardless of what, how, or why Cessnas end up on the killing floor of the courtroom, the single-engine Cessnas seem, for airplanes that are semi-mass produced, to be a pretty tough group of airplanes.

I'm fairly sure that no one at Wichita expected these things to be flying regularly over twenty-five years after the aluminum was cut. Sure, a very few airplanes have given a very lot of problems. Some have smacked the earth really hard. Nevertheless, when given the care that an airplane demands, the vast majority have proven to be exceptionally reliable airplanes.

Picture owning a 1977 Ford, or any other car of that vintage. How much do you think it would cost to run it at seventy-five percent power up to yesterday. Right!

And you don't own a '77 anything today with the expectation that it will perform like a 1993 anything, do you?

I guess what all my pontificating is about, is that buying a small, single-engine airplane ten to twenty years old will not be like buying the latest wizz-bang fresh off the dealer's shelf. But ownership can be a rewarding experience, if you are prepared to spend some time and money to keep your plane up. Or the plane can be nothing but a money drain that stays tied down to the earth for all its life.

We've all seen the airplanes tied down at an airport that have flat tires, faded paint, missing panels, and a family of something small living beneath the cowling. These airplanes are probably out of annual, with the engine run out and the owner out of interest.

They look like a bargain to a would-be, first-time owner. Just fill the tires, clean her up, rebuild the engine and prop, throw a paint job at 'er, get a fresh annual, oh yes, put in some avionics that work, back into the panel, and she'll be right up there with the new ones. Only cost 'bout twice as much as a low-time model that doesn't have to be remanufactured to fly. Be careful. If in doubt, ask someone who is currently flying the same airplane that you lust after.

Where were we? Oh yes, the Hawk XP and its performance.

The Hawk XP can be expected to get off the runway, with a full load, in 100ft less than a 172. Once trimmed for cruise, count on an airspeed around 125kt, depending on prop and throttle setting.

Remember, keep the XP happy by feeding it 10gph. Lean to proper mixture at altitude. Don't try to make it run on 8gph or you'll get on a first name basis with your mechanic and the parts guy will send you Christmas cards.

Keep up on all the repairs. Go fly someplace interesting.

When it's time to move up from the Hawk XP, you might even make some money on the deal.

C-172 Hawk XP Rating
Investment: #2
Utility: #4
Popularity: #3

Cessna 172 Cutlass and Cutlass RG

The Cutlass RG is Cessna's idea of a training aircraft for transitioning up from a 172 to an airplane with retractable gear: not much more than a 172 with a 180hp engine, constant-speed prop, and gear that tucks away for a 120kt cruise—not a large speed increase for all that much more complexity over a 172.

Most FBOs that I talked to consider that the Cutlass RG was intended to be only a trainer and shouldn't be considered as anything else. FBOs that operate 152s and 172s as primary trainers can move their students into a slightly more powerful plane that fits the FAA's designation of a "complex" aircraft by

---

C-172 Hawk XP Specifications

Engine, 1978: Continental IO-360-K of 195hp with 1,500-hour TBO
Maximum Weight, 1978: 2,550lb
Fuel Capacity: 52gal
Maximum Cruise Speed: 130kt at 80% power and 6,000ft
Range: 480nm, 3.7 hours with 49gal usable fuel at 6,000ft
Rate of Climb: 870fpm
Service Ceiling: 17,000ft
Takeoff Performance: 800ft ground roll; 1,360ft over 50ft obstacle
Landing Performance: 620ft ground roll; 1,360ft over 50ft obstacle
Stall Speed with Flaps Down, Power Off: 46kt
Standard Empty Weight: 1,531lb
Useful Load: 1,019lb
Wingspan: 35ft, 10in
Length: 27ft, 2in
Height: 8ft, 9.5in

stepping up to the RG. Retractable gear, a constant speed prop or 200hp and above will fit an airplane into the complex category. Those of you who want to pick up some speed by picking up the gear should be aware that a Cutlass RG only cruises about 5–10kt faster than the 172. A Piper Arrow will easily outrun a Cutlass RG and the Hawk XP or the basic 172 doesn't have the added maintenance costs associated with a constant speed prop and retractable gear. The Cutlass RG is a good trainer and should be looked at in that light only. If you teach flying and need a complex airplane for your students, then a 1980 to 1985 Cutlass RG in the $45,000–60,000k range would be a good buy. As in all other smaller Cessnas, the Cutlass RG will return a large percentage of its purchase price when it comes time to resell the airplane, if it is properly maintained and kept looking good.

There is another version of the Cutlass that isn't seen very often and that's the straight-leg model. It fits in between the Hawk XP, with 195hp and the 172 with 160hp. From the outside the differences between the 172 and the Cutlass fixed gear are insignificant. What you mainly get is a 172 with a 180hp O-360 Lycoming engine, possibly the most bullet proof motor ever made, with a fixed-pitch prop hung out front. What you also get is a very rare airplane, I could only find fewer than thirty registered with the FAA as of mid-1993. Only made in 1983 and 1984, it sold new for an average price of $75,000 with a full instrument package and a 62gal fuel capacity in a wet wing. The wet wing idea eliminates the standard fuel tank, using the wing as a fuel tank. Today a Cutlass with original logs, good paint and interior and no damage history will bring $55,000. For comparison, the last 195hp Hawk XP, built in 1981, will set you back about the same amount of money for fifteen more horsepower and a slightly higher cruise speed. The biggest problem with a Cutlass fixed-gear is that the people who own the thirty or so airplanes still around know what they have and plan to keep them. I was unable to find any fixed-gear Cutlass for sale anywhere. Good luck!

C-172 Cutlass & Cutlass RG Typical Specifications
Engine, 1980: Lycoming O-360-F1A6 of 180hp with 2,000-hour TBO
Maximum Weight, 1,980: 2,650lb
Fuel Capacity: 66gal
Maximum Cruise Speed: 138kt at 75% power
All Other Specs Similar to Cessna 172

Cutlass and Cutlass RG Rating
Investment: #3
Utility: #4
Popularity: #3 (Cutlass RG)
#1 (Cutlass)

Cessna 177 Cardinal and Cardinal RG

Just when you thought you knew how to fly a Cessna, along comes the Cardinal. With its lack of struts and forward-mounted windscreen, it looks like no other small Cessna flying. Not only doesn't it look like a 172, but it also takes off, flies, and lands unlike the strutted Cessnas.

The wing was mounted farther back on the fuselage of the 177 than on other Cessnas. In order to ensure enough control without a horizontal stabilizer and elevator system much larger than planned, Cessna built in a single, movable surface as a "stabilator." In making that modification, the major change was the installation of inverted slots near the leading edge to keep the wing from stalling at high angles of attack.

After some heavy-handed pilots managed to tear off the Cardinal's nose gear or sand down the tail on landing, Cessna went back to the drawing board to make the 177 fly like all the other Cessnas that people were accustomed to driving on and off the runway.

Cessna found that the stabilator was stalling out when the airplane was in a full nose-up attitude. The airplane hadn't been intended to be flown onto the runway with the trim all the way back and the nose pointed at the sun. However, that's what was happening.

The Cardinal first appeared in 1967 with a 150hp engine and fixed gear. This wasn't

Two versions of the Cessna 177 Cardinal, one
fixed gear, the other a retractable.

enough power for a 2,500lb airplane, especially one that looked so much faster than a braced-wing 172, so in late 1968 a 180hp Continental was fitted. About 1,000 of the 150hp 1968 models were built.

Cessna wisely decided to add a little more go by installing a 180hp Lycoming, with a constant-speed prop coming along in the seventies.

The Cardinal RG appeared in 1971 with a constant speed prop and 200hp under the cowl. The book says that when the gear goes up the 177RG smokes along 18kt faster than its fixed-gear relative. Not what I've seen, but maybe all the ones I've flown have been slow versions of the RG. About all the difference on the airspeed indicator at 7,500ft is 10–15kt.

Anyone who has watched a single-engine, retractable Cessna on takeoff has a pretty good idea of the convolutions the airplane goes through to get the wheels into the fuselage. If you are contemplating buying a retractable Cessna single and you're not familiar with the gear system, go to the nearest airport on any weekend and watch the Cessna RGs do funny things. Do make it a point to see if the Power-Pack has been rebuilt in the last five years. It doesn't hold a whole lot of hydraulic fluid. If the red stuff runs down the belly instead of to the actuators, the end of your flight will be punctuated by loud, expensive, grinding noises. Also, check to see when the gear locks were last adjusted and whether the micro-switches on the uplocks have been replaced. Mine hadn't. Fourteen hundred dollars and a week in the shop took care of that little oversight.

The 1973 Cardinal got a new model of the trusty Lycoming engine incorporating an oil filter for the first time. Fuel capacity was upped to 61gal at the same time. I'd probably look for a C-177 built after this date. In 1974, according to another book, the biggest change was a larger coat hangar, and there was no price increase.

The early 150hp models of the 177 don't bring quite as much on the used market. Usually a 1968 can be found in the $25,000 range, with the 1969 bringing $32,000 or more, mostly because of the bigger engine. If I were going to spring for a Cardinal and $25,000 was my budget, I'd try to come up with the extra money for the later airplane with 30hp more. Granted, 30hp does not sound like a lot more power. But trust me; in this case, you

---

C-177 and C-177RG Specifications

Engine:
1967—Lycoming O-320-E2D of 150hp with 2,000-hour TBO
1968—Lycoming O-360-A2F of 180hp with 2,000-hour TBO
1971—Lycoming O-360-A1B6 of 200hp with 2,000-hour TBO (first RG)
Maximum Weight:
1967 C-177—2,350lb
1968 C-177—2,500lb
1971 C-177RG—2,800lb
Fuel Capacity: 49–61gal
Maximum Cruise:
150hp C-177—145mph
180hp C-177—150mph
200hp C-177RG—160mph
Maximum Cruise Speed, C-177: 130kt at 75% power and 10,000ft
Maximum Cruise Speed, C-177RG: 148kt at 75% power and 7,000ft
Range, C-177: 535nm, 4.2 hours with 49gal usable fuel
Range, C-177RG: 715nm, 4.9 hours with 60gal usable fuel
Rate of Climb, C-177: 840fpm
Rate of Climb, C-177RG: 925fpm
Service Ceiling, C-177: 14,600ft
Service Ceiling, C-177RG: 17,100ft
Takeoff Performance, C-177: 750ft ground roll; 1,400ft over 50ft obstacle
Takeoff Performance, C-177RG: 890ft ground roll; 1,585ft over 50ft obstacle
Landing Performance, C-177: ground roll 600ft; 1,220ft over 50ft obstacle
Landing Performance, C-177RG: ground roll 730fttft; 1,350ft over 50ft obstacle
Stall Speed with Flaps Down, Power Off, C-177: 40kt
Stall Speed with Flaps Down, Power Off, C-177RG: 50kt
Maximum Weight, C-177: 2,500lb
Maximum Weight, C-177RG: 2,800lb
Standard Empty Weight, C-177: 1,533lb
Standard Empty Weight, C-177RG: 1,707lb
Maximum Useful Load, C-177: 967lb
Maximum Useful Load, C-177RG: 1,093lb
Wingspan: 35ft, 6in
Length: 27ft, 3in
Height: 8ft, 7in

won't be disappointed. Also, at resale, everything you spend will come back.

One of the better selling points of a Cardinal to anyone who has flown Piper Archers or Warriors is the four-foot-wide doors on each side of the airplane. If you're used to climbing up the wing to get in the pilot's seat before the passenger can fill the right seat, the Cardinal will be a real treat. The passengers you unceremoniously stuffed in the back seats will really appreciate the Cardinal's ease of entry. It's still hard to picture anyone in a skirt getting into the back seat of a Piper four-place single with any amount of grace. Or me either, for that matter.

Once in the Cardinal, with the seat moved forward into flying position, the increased visibility becomes apparent. The wing doesn't block the view of the runway when turning base to final as in some other high-wing planes. Be sure to check for the seat retention pin in the seat rails. This will keep the seat from running full back if the pin lock fails.

If picking up the gear and flying like the big guys appeals to you, by all means go buy a Cardinal RG. Hard to find a prettier airplane in the sky. When you've checked the paperwork, read the logs, and you're finally ready to look at that 177RG, take a flashlight. Don't just sit in the seat and play with the knobs and switches. Move the seat back to its full travel. Or better yet, pull it out altogether; it comes out easily. Lie down on the floor and look up above the rudder pedals. Check the master cylinders mounted about four inches up for leaking hydraulic fluid. Also, if the airplane is so equipped, look at the Power-Pack. This collection of hoses, rods, and tank is the heart of the retractable-gear system.

If, on the other hand, getting there is half the fun, and large maintenance bills don't excite you, stick with the fixed-gear 180hp version.

Most of the Cardinals for sale in the last couple of months (January through April 1993) show a lot of the newer goodies in the panel. Finding a 177 with dual King navcoms, loran, Mode C transponder, autopilot, intercom, and full IFR equipment for $35,000 to $45,000 seems to be fairly easy. The *Retail Aircraft Appraisal Guide* shows a high of $62,000 for a 1978 177RG and a low of $20,000 for a 150hp 1968 Cardinal straight-leg. With a spread of $42,000, if a Cardinal is in your plans, there's a lot of range to look.

C-177 and C-177 RG Rating
Investment: #4
Utility: #4
Popularity: #3

Chapter 4

The Big Singles

Cessna 182 Skylane, Turbo Skylane, and Turbo Skylane RG

The Cessna 182 Skylane is Cessna's smallest true four-place airplane. Even though the 182 bears a similarity to the 172 Skyhawk at first glance, actually the two airplanes are quite a bit different. The Skylane is a heavier airplane by 500lb and has some more sophisticated features with which you will have to become familiar.

The 182 has a constant-speed prop and cowl flaps that must be mastered. Usually 5–8 hours of checkout are required. The 182 will easily carry a much larger load than the 172. It's not an airplane in which the student pilot should begin his flight training because

A tall Cessna. This is an early C-182 up on amphibious floats. Sometimes the floats will double the value of an airplane, true with this particular airplane.

Turning the prop through on a preflight inspection. Does the engine turn smoothly? Can you feel the compression as the pistons come up to top dead center (TDC)? This is the time to locate problems, not thirty minutes into the flight.

it's a lot of airplane to master while trying to figure out how to read a chart, fly the airplane, and decipher all those funny gauges. The Skylane is an all around cross-country airplane with all four seats occupied and a healthy load of fuel and baggage on board. With a useful load of well over a half ton, weight and balance is not so critical as it is on the 182's little brothers. This doesn't mean that if you don't have to run at the door more than three times to close it, you're under maximum weight. To the contrary, with all the widgets, radios, intercoms, and general gadgets owners like to stuff in the panel of the average 182, the empty weight can easily run 200–300lb over published figures. With a full load of fuel in the long-range tanks weighing around 500lb and four well-fed people on board, you probably will find that the airplane is on the wrong side of maximum weight by a large amount. Usually by this time the Center of Gravity (CG) and balance have gone out the window, too. Get outside the weight and balance envelope, and you become a test pilot. No thanks.

However, with some attention paid to what goes into the cabin and fuel tanks, the 182 will do a good job of hauling a pilot plus three passengers over 500 miles with IFR reserves. This works out to about 3–4 hours in

C-182 Specifications

Engine:
1956—Continental O-470-L of 230hp with 1,500-hour TBO
1962—Continental O-470-R of 230hp with 1500-hour TBO
1975—Continental O-470-S of 230hp with 1500-hour TBO
1977—Continental O-470-U of 230hp with 2,000-hour TBO
1981—Continental O-540-L3C5D with 2,000-hour TBO
1978 RG—Continental O-540-J3C5D with 2,000-hour TBO

Maximum Weight:
1956 C-182: 2,550lb
1957 C-182A: 2,650lb
1962 C-182E: 2,800lb
1977 C-182Q: 2,950lb
1978 C-182R, 182RG, TR-182: 3,100lb
1981—C-182R, T-182: 3,100lb takeoff, 2,950lb landing
Fuel Capacity: 60–92gal

Maximum Cruise:
1957—139kt
1977–1979 R-182—160kt
Maximum Cruise: 144kt at 75% power and 7,000ft
Range: 475nm, 3.4 hours with 56gal usable fuel at 6,500ft
Range: 670nm, 4.7 hours with 75gal usable fuel at 6,500ft
Rate of Climb at Sea Level: 890fpm
Service Ceiling: 17,700ft
Takeoff Performance: 705ft ground roll; 1,350ft over 50ft obstacle,
Landing Performance: 590ft ground roll; 1,350ft over 50ft obstacle
Stall Speed with Flaps Up, Power Off: 56kt
Stall Speed with Flaps Down, Power Off: 50kt
Maximum Weight: 2,950lb
Standard Empty Weight, Skylane I,707lb
Standard Empty Weight, Skylane II: 1,771lb
Maximum Useful Load, Skylane I: 243lb
Maximum Useful Load, Skylane II: 1,179lb
Wing Span: 35ft, 10in
Length: 28ft, 2in
Height: 9ft, 1.5in

Fueling a 182. Take the time to climb the ladder and check the fuel level after filling. Are the tanks filled to the top or did he stop one inch below the filler neck? The difference can be measured in gallons that might make a difference on a long flight.

the air—one more hour than my bladder can stand, even with only one cup of airport coffee.

As far as visualizing what kind of distance you can plan on an average nonstop trip, my 1971 C-182 would make the trip from Tucson, Arizona, to San Jose, California, in just over 4 hours, depending on head-winds. Ground speed would vary according to the wind, but I have found that 135kt is real close to actual performance, regardless of what all the handbooks and advertising dream sheets had to say. Usual fuel burn was in the 13gph range. I had to fly at 11,500ft to get over some of the taller rocks on the route, so the 182 spent a lot of time climbing.

Going over the Sierra Nevadas in California, it was nice to have the O-470 engine up in front, with 235hp on tap. Once, crossing the Sierras going east out of California, I found myself in a 2,500fpm downdraft with the throttle and prop all the way up to the panel. Did make for an interesting moment or two, but I had around 3,000ft between me and the sharp stuff below, so I was able to work out of the downhill ride without a problem.

Another tip when it comes to the 182. With one person aboard and half-full to full tanks, the airplane wants to land nose first. Sometimes this makes for a logbook entry like "Changed nose gear and strut; straightened firewall." Beware of any 182 that is advertised with a C-206 nose gear. The odds are that it played wheelbarrow one time too hard

By 1962, the C-182's lines were finalized and the 1984 model looks pretty much the same as this early Skylane. *Cessna Aircraft Company*

Hard to see because of the old picture, but check the rear window treatment on this early Cessna. *Cessna Aircraft Company*

Count the antennas on this 182. The owner has upgraded the panel to a full set of solid-state avionics. The strings on the rudder and elevator are for static discharge, keeps static electricity from building up on the airframe.

and the front gear and prop got significantly altered. Not that this can't be repaired. However, either you or the mechanic who does the prepurchase inspection should take a good look at the firewall for wrinkles. With the average age of these airplanes hitting twenty years or more, the chance of a hard-nose landing, with the resulting damage, becomes more possible. The cure for a nose-gear arrival is to treat the 182 like a heavier airplane and roll in full nose-up trim just before touchdown.

The prices for Cessna 182s run all the way from $4,500 for an early model with a run-out engine and a wooden door to $89,900 for a 1983 T-182RG loaded to the high-water mark with three-axis autopilot, slaved Horizontal Situation Indicator (HSI), and just about anything else that will fit in the panel or not hang too far out the door. As with all the rest of the planes, you pretty much get what you pay for in a 182.

One of the other problem areas to be aware of when dealing with a 182 is water in the fuel bladders. Most everyone familiar with the aircraft knows about the problem by now. However, if you are a first-time buyer and not real familiar with the airplane, the best method, if you suspect water, is to rock the wings before checking the fuel drains. There was an Airworthiness Directive (AD) issued a while back that advised the pilot to "rock wings vigorously." This normally eliminates any water in the fuel. Another way to go is to have the wings opened up so that all the wrinkles can be smoothed out of the bladders. Not a cheap

fix, though. I'd probably watch real closely for water contamination, shake the wings if you even imagine a problem, and make sure the fuel caps are watertight. Another AD concerns fuel-cap sealing and water contamination, covering the problem in greater detail. Always check all ADs on the year and model that you are lusting over, as you can get carried away during the sale and forget to check every piece of paperwork connected to the airplane.

Yes, you can. I did it . . . and then I got to pay for it.

A stock Cessna ARC radio panel in a 182. Everything from the audio panel at the top to the autopilot at the bottom is as it left the factory. It is rather unusual to see a fifteen-year-old panel that has remained untouched. This is another airplane worth owning.

A 182 taxis under the tower on its way to run-up.

Not the way to treat a 182. This airplane has sat on flat tires and has been sporting a plywood door for the ten years I've been flying out of this airport. It's now only good for parts, but the county has seized it for delinquent tie-down fees, and it's going through court for legal disposition.

An unusual conversion on a 182 frame. Called a Wren 260, it is a completely remanufactured airframe, larger 260hp engine (over the standard 235hp), a STOL kit and flyable canards on the nose. This one just lifted off after an under-500ft run, check the shadow for the nose canards.

One nice thing about owning a 182 is that they aren't getting any cheaper as time goes on. If you purchase a good one, maintain it well. Keep it looking good. Stay ahead of the chintzy plastic trim parts; the odds are better than even that you'll show a profit on the resale. Of course, the airplane won't ex-actly be free to fly. If you figure about $75–$80 dollars per hour operating and impound cost, you won't be far off. Most people have a hard time putting money in an account with an eye towards maintenance and future engine or prop overhaul. However, if you treat maintenance and repairs as

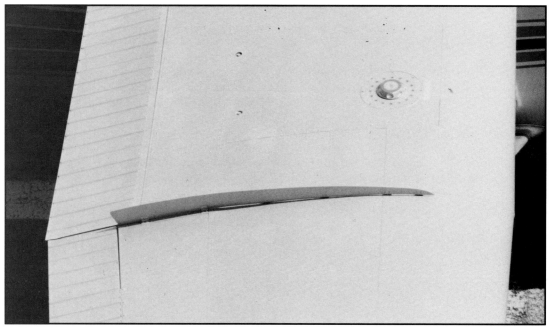

A shot of the top of the wing of the Wren 260,
showing the STOL stall fence and an uprated fuel
cap to keep water out of the tanks.

Probably the most unusual aspect of the Wren 260
Conversion, the canards. Easy to see that they are
operational.

an ongoing expense that you'll have for as long as you fly the airplane, and put the money somewhere out of sight or hard to touch, when the big repair bills arrive it won't seem so much like the IRS came to call. In today's market, hoisting a rebuilt engine onto the front of a Skylane can easily run into five figures. Also, another point to keep in mind. If the cowling over the engine says "Turbo," figure on adding another $3,000–$4,000 in additional cost for the turbocharger and related bits and pieces that will have to be replaced when the engine is done.

The turbocharged 182s require more maintenance, and have higher operating costs, because they operate at higher temperatures. Heat is the big killer in these engines. The turbo maintains its rated horsepower at a higher altitude by forcing air under 6–10psi of pressure into the motor. As the air is squeezed into the intake manifold, its temperature rises along with the pressure. Probably 75 percent of nonscheduled maintenance

Above and following page
This sequence shows the "ruptured duck" operation of Cessna's retractable gear system. The system is actually quite reliable when set up properly. Mine didn't go down only once! My fault—not that of the airplane.

A 1964 Skylane is the run-up area. *Cessna Aircraft Company*

on a T-182 is directly related to its turbocharged engine. You gotta pay to breathe deep and fly high.

One of the ways to help beat the heat and make everything from exhaust manifolds to valves last longer is to mount an intercooler on the engine. If you have a Supplemental Type Certificate (STC) for the installation of an intercooler on the particular Continental engine in your 182, consider putting one in. It will more than pay for itself over the projected life of the engine. Most turbocharged engines have the cylinders pulled and rebuilt after about 800 to 900 operating hours. Usually the pistons and valves have to be replaced,

and the cylinders have to be rebored. The airplane is tied up for one to two weeks at the minimum while the engine is apart. Often the cylinders have to be sent out to be rebuilt, since most repair shops don't have the facilities to do the necessary machine work, and that takes additional time. A lot of the engine wear is due to the increased stress and heat load imposed by the turbocharger. Anything that can be done to reject the heat from the incoming charge will only help the engine live. The intercooler mounts between the turbo high-pressure discharge and the engine intake. Its purpose is to cool the incoming charge, which in turn keeps the temperature

A 1963 Skylane banks away from the photo plane.
Cessna Aircraft Company

Cessna 206 Stationair, the pick-up truck of the fleet. By the lack of wheel fairings and addition of anti-chip on the horizontal stabilizer, this bird looks like it gets in the dirt a lot.

down in the combustion chamber. Less heat equals longer engine life.

When you up the ante to a retractable 182RG, figure on a 20–30 percent increase in the per-hour cost—directly related to gear operation. Without going into the whys and hows of a single-engine Cessna gear system, the best way I can explain the operation of the gear is to tell you to go to your nearest airport and watch a 182RG, 210, or 337 take off. Once you've seen the motions the gear goes through to retract into the fuselage on a high-wing airplane, the increased cost per hour will become quite apparent. Also (if you need more convincing), replacing the 0.25in flare swivel-fitting on the brake line, which rotates every time the gear cycles, runs about $310 without labor (and that was in 1991). Plus there are two on each aircraft.

How do you think I learned that piece of trivia? Yup, both of them!

Don't get me wrong. If you want to take four people up high and go 160kt with the gear sucked up like a real airplane, it would be hard to beat a turbo, retractable Skylane (TR-182). All in all, a Cessna 182, whatever the model or year, is one of the better choices you can make when shopping for a four-place aircraft.

C-182 Rating
Investment: #1
Utility: #2
Popularity: #1

Cessna 205, 206, Skywagon and Stationair

Skywagon, Super Skywagon, Stationair, or Utility Stationair—whatever name Cessna's big workhorse goes by, it's one of the most popular load haulers on the used-airplane market.

Starting in 1962 with the 205 Skywagon, Cessna set out to manufacture a single-engined airplane that would carry in excess of a half ton into some pretty rugged areas. A lot of the 205s and 206s found their way to the cold end of the North American continent, where they were put to work hauling everything from gold ore to tractor parts. The first time I saw a forklift shoveling a bright yellow

Caterpillar diesel engine head into the double doors of a 206 on a gravel strip up in Denali National Park in Alaska, I kept waiting for the bottom of the airplane to end up in the gravel of the runway. No such luck! The mine workers cinched it down (with what looked like a net capable of holding Godzilla) and slammed the doors shut, and the pilot had the 206 off the gravel runway in less than 1,000ft. Impressive? You bet! Since I was just a lowly student pilot at the time who thought a 152 was an airplane, you can imagine my thoughts as I watched a single-engined Cessna take off with what amounted to an entire 152 as cargo. I had a ways to go, yet, before I was ready for that trick. I mean, what would you do if the load shifted aft in turbulence? Try to turn into a helicopter, I imagine.

C-205 and C-206 Specifications

Engine, C-205 and C-206: Continental IO-520-F of 300hp at 2,850rpm, 285hp at 2,700rpm (maximum continuous)

Engine, Turbo Skywagon: Continental TSIO-520-M of 310hp at 2,700rpm, 285hp at 2,600rpm (maximum continuous)

Maximum Weight: 3,612lb ramp, 3,600lb takeoff or landing

Maximum Cruise:
Sea Level—156kt
75% power at 6,500ft—147kt
Turbo—174kt at 17,000ft
80% power at 20,000ft—152kt
Rate of Climb at Sea Level: 920fpm
Service Ceiling: 14,800ft
Takeoff Performance: 900ft ground roll; 1,395ft over 50ft obstacle
Takeoff Performance, Floatplane: 1,835ft water run; 2,820ft over 50ft obstacle
Landing Performance: 735ft ground roll; 1,395ft over 50ft obstacle
Landing Performance, Floatplane: 780ft water run; 1,675ft over 50ft obstacle
Stall Speed with Flaps Up, Power Off: 62kt
Stall Speed with Flaps Down, Power Off: 54kt
Maximum Load: 1,632lb (Stationair) to 1,795lb (Utility with one seat)
Standard Empty Weight, Landplane: 1,817lb (Utility Stationair) to 1,980lb (Stationair)
Standard Empty Weight, Floatplane: 2,178lb (Utility Stationair) to 2,321lb (Stationair)
Wing Span: 35ft, 10in
Length: 28ft, 3in
Height: 9ft, 3.5in

The first Cessna 206, introduced in 1965, was called the Super Skywagon, not to confuse it with the other half-dozen or so names it would pick up along the way.

It was a direct descendent of the 205 with numerous changes to the airframe to beef it up for the missions it would be called upon to fly, usually with a heavy load in back. The fuselage was strengthened in the floor area to increase load capability, and a 3.5ft double door was added so that heavy and bulky cargo could be loaded. I remember hearing stories, back in the seventies, of a baby grand piano being loaded through those doors. Probably a publicity stunt, but I did see a picture or two . . .

The 206 used the same wing that appeared on the 210 in 1964 with almost 20ft of

flap and Frise ailerons with increased chord. This allowed the pilot to retain control authority when the 206 was flying slow and heavy, giving better feel on approach.

The Turbo Super Skywagon was added to the line-up in 1966, giving the normally aspirated 206 a horsepower increase going out of high-altitude airports on a hot day.

Turbocharging is used in two ways. First, the total output of the engine can be raised by as much as thirty percent at sea level (as in the Ford Mustang SVO, whose engine started out as a lowly 115hp Pinto engine; it was reborn as a 205hp BMW basher that spins along at 135mph).

Second, the turbo will maintain the engine's rated power output up at altitude. The turbo adds power by compressing the intake

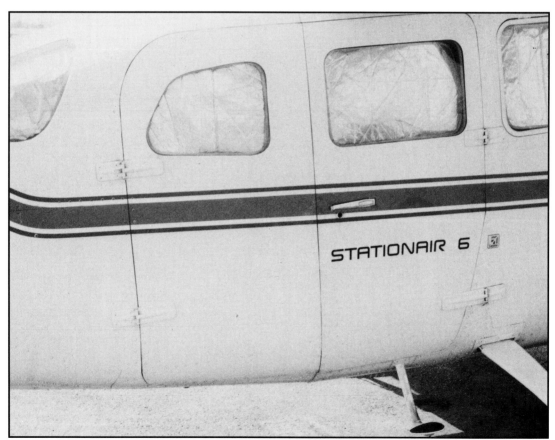

"And the piano goes in here." The cargo doors on a 206. Easy to see how, with the doors removed, this would make a good skydiver airplane. Stack them in and throw them out!

charge before it reaches the engine, so the total amount of gas-air mixture in the cylinders is increased. At altitudes in the high teens, where there is a decrease in air density, the denser fuel-air mixture helps maintain cruise power. The normally aspirated engine would have its tongue hanging out. The turbo engine in the 300hp Cessnas reaches 174kt at 17,000ft. It will cruise at around 165kt at 20,000ft, while the standard engine peaks at 7,500ft.

In real life terms, this means you can load five large humans, their dog, and enough luggage for an extended vacation, then light the fire and go nonstop from San Francisco to Seattle in three-and-a-half hours or so, depending on the wind.

Good idea: Remember to bring along oxygen, though, or it could be a short trip at altitude.

What the turbo normally was employed to do was to help a C-206 lift off a rough field strip with a heavy load in the back. A corollary to this is that if you are in the market for a 206, with plans to use it for something sane like skydiving, it would behoove you to spend the time and money to ensure that your intended choice didn't spend a greater

An older 206. Sells for more now than when it was new.

An Argentina-registered Super Skywagon set up as a sprayer. *Cessna Aircraft Company*

part of its life bouncing in and out of what passes for airstrips in the more remote areas of the world, with a load on board that would send a camel to its knees. Let's face it; some of these aircraft have been used as tractors for a good part of their life. I'm not saying that if the airplane saw duty in Alaska as a glorified mining implement, that it hasn't been well maintained. But the last one I saw come out of the North had 6,700 hours on the airframe, and the motor-mount bolts had been run on and off so many times that the threads on the studs were starting to take a polish.

Of course, if you don't mind a little wear and tear on your airplane, and you'd like a project that will keep you away from home

nights, by all means buy one in that condition. They're all built like bridges, and if the one you buy hasn't been on its top or had an engine block fall through the cargo floor, you could end up with a good airplane after some work.

But bring money.

Speaking of money, the price for these aircraft has risen steadily for the last three or four years. A fairly well-equipped 1979 206, originally listing for $59,000, is now advertised in *Trade-A-Plane* for an asking price of $87,750. This is for a 1,050 total time airframe and engine (TTAF&E), one owner, always hangared, fully IFR airplane. The ad says it has new paint, a new annual, and has never been scratched—and "no bargaining."

Sure a nice way to play on the water. A Skywagon on floats up in Canada. *Cessna Aircraft Company*

Bring money.

On the other side of the bank account is a 1964 U-206 with 5,800 hours total time, 1,040 hours on the latest engine, very little avionics, tired paint, and heavy-duty nose gear. (Usually means someone tore off the original wheel while playing wheelbarrow on a dirt strip.) And the owner says it's ugly (really!). But he's only asking for $34,900. With some shrewd bargaining, you could probably knock him down a buck or two.

Bring money.

Actually, after looking over what's in the trade papers in the 205/206 market, there are quite a few aircraft for sale with under 2,000 hours on the airframe and on the first go around with the engine. Most of them seem to be well equipped in the avionics department—with loran, late-model radios, and autopilots helping to fill the panel. Probably a lot of the low-time aircraft have spent their lives hauling a family of five on vacations, and they are clean airplanes in mint condition.

More of those cardboard boxes ready to disappear into an early Skywagon. *Cessna Aircraft Company*

Remember, take the time and effort to have a reliable FBO check out the airplane fully prior to purchase. It's too late to complain about the missing rivets in the belly pan after your name is on the registration.

You think I kid! I saw one come through a few years ago with a brand sparkling new Imron paint job and the smoothest finish on the belly I'd ever seen. Looked real clean. The new owner was proud of how slick his airplane was. Real slick sitting on the ramp in the sun.

Turns out that a few rivets were missing from the bottom of the airplane.

About 150!

Wonder how it spent its time since new? You don't think it ever took off overloaded, do you? Flexed a little on some rough landings, maybe? Takes a pretty good bounce to shear rivets off a fuselage.

As I say, if a plane has a high-time airframe, look real hard. Not that it couldn't be

a good airplane; just be sure.

I ran across a 1969 206 on amphibian floats in Seattle, with 6,300 hours TTAF&E that looked like it had just come from the factory at Wichita the day before. Sitting on a set of amphib floats, it reached almost 15ft in the air. Lots of airplane. I personally think that a 205/206 floatplane is one of the best looking aircraft in the sky; I've wanted one for a long time. After talking to the owner and talking price, I realized that I could either own his airplane or pay the rent and buy food. Sure was a nice airplane, though.

Checking out the ADs for the 205/206 series of Cessnas shows all the usual problems related to the seat locking, fuel contamination, and loss of engine power from parts ingestion connected with the single-engine airplanes. However, many of the ADs that relate to the Stationair and Skywagon don't apply to the other singles, and some of the problems are expensive fixes. There are a

I always wonder what the guy in the photo did to get put in the cheap seats in Cessna photos. I guess this trick is one way of showing that there are three rows of seats in this C-205. *Cessna Aircraft Company*

number of ADs that cover loss of oil pressure due to failure of components on the turbo, namely failure of thrust-bearing pins. One particular AD covers cracks and loose bolts that could cause the fin and rudder to part company with the rest of the airplane—a fairly serious problem, since not many airplanes will fly very well without a tail. A long, expensive list of fixes. They're easier to read about and check before buying an airplane, than to discover after you own it. But then, no one's ever accused these planes of being cheap to own.

As I've said above . . . bring money.

If an amphibious or straight float-equipped airplane is in your future, be prepared to pay up to eighty percent over the cost of a landplane. A set of Edo or Wiplane floats can easily add $35,000 to $40,000 to the overall price of the 206. However, if you plan to fly in Alaska, Canada, or the northwest territories, having a Cessna 206 that can function on water as well as land is the only way to fly. Sometimes literally, as airports are few and far between on the cold end of the continent.

Flying off water is a whole new experience in aviation. Teaching seaplane opera-

The Business end of a 210 Centurion. Cowl flaps, retractable gear, turbocharging, three-bladed prop, all add up to a very complex single-engined airplane.

tions is beyond the scope of this book, but I'll list two items you should consider. One, an additional type rating is required for water operations. And two, when you do operate off the water, remember that once the engine starts, you move. There are no brakes on a floatplane.

One of the supreme pleasures in my life was a flight in southern Washington state, going down the Columbia River in a 206 on floats. We were about 20 to 30ft above the water, flying about 130mph, just keeping the left wingtip off the north bank of the river and watching the afternoon sunlight run down the water in front of us. Every so often the pilot would let the floats settle down until they would lightly kick up enough spray to leave a rainbow rooster tail behind us.

Later that evening, I lay in a hammock tied between two trees about 50ft up the riverbank, watching the 206, silhouetted by the campfire, slowly rocking up and down in the current. Thinking about the fresh fish dinner that had just passed, and supported by an authentic Columbia River-chilled bottle of white zinfandel from the Napa Valley of California, I figured all was right with the world. I could probably spend a large portion of my life in that way. Listening to the river gently slap against the floats put me to sleep faster than ten pages of a detective paperback.

We continued for another three days,

Time to go. Full power, watch the manifold pressure, stay on the centerline, correct for a slight cross-wind, turn on the transponder to Mode C, watch the airspeed and don't run over the 152 that took off in front of you. Sounds tough, doesn't it? After hundreds of hours, it happens as easy as driving a 172.

and by the end of the trip I was ready to send a thank-you note to Cessna. A very nice way to fly.

C-205 and C-206 Rating
Investment: #1
Utility: #1
Popularity: #3

Cessna 210 Centurion

To the first-time buyer, the Cessna 210 Centurion might just look like a 182RG with a little more go and a bit more useful load. However, the 210 is an all-new design from the wheels to the wings. A lot more airplane than first meets the eye. It first appeared in the fall of 1959 as a 1960 model, aimed at a market that was more upscale than that for the smaller retractables. The first models had a 260hp Continental engine and a gross weight of 2,900lb. But by 1986, the 210 had 325hp and weighed 4,100lb sitting on the ramp. It had grown into a high-altitude, pressurized, turbocharged, 200mph powerhouse.

The Centurion 210R, which started out in 1960 as a $15,000 airplane, listed in the January issue of the *N.A.D.A. Retail Appraisal Guide* for $233,000. The pressurized version ter than even that you won't lose any money owning a 210 if you take reasonable care of it. However, a lot of the cost of flying a high-performance airplane comes from keeping it in the air. With the current costs of everything from fuel to light bulbs on an upward curve, it would be hard to hang an average per-hour cost on owning a 210 or any 200mph airplane. You can be reasonably sure that it will cost just slightly more than you think you can afford.

As an example, an FBO at San Jose Airport just installed a factory remanufactured engine in a 1982 Turbo 210 for a cost of more than $43,000. This included all the bits and pieces that are part of what's called "Firewall Forward Remanufactured" (FF Reman). Everything from the prop to the vacuum pumps was either replaced with new parts or rebuilt to factory-new condition. When you factor this into a 1,600-hour TBO, it works out to $27 per hour just for engine replacement. Figure in an annual inspection cost of anywhere from $2,500 to a whole lot more, a fuel cost per hour around $35–38, and maintenance costs in the $40 dollar per hour range, and you get a general idea as to what you'll spend to own a fairly low-time 210.

Lest you think the ongoing maintenance estimate is high, let me give you a personal example. Last year my C-337 Skymaster (actually a 1967 Air Force O-2A I restored over three years—but that's another interesting story) decided it didn't want to put its gear up all the way. Lucky for me, the wheels stayed in the down-and-locked position, so getting back to the hangar was only mildly exciting. Next step was into the shop and up into the air on jacks.

It turned out that we needed to replace three micro-switches on the gear. Of course, this entailed jacking the airplane up almost three feet so that the gear could be swung and tested. This was a semiscary proposition that took time and two mechanics plus me. If you want to increase your blood pressure and test your cardiac system, go help shop mechanics lift your 3,700lb twin high enough off the ground so that the gear can swing free twelve inches off the concrete. Some of the creaks and groans came from the airplane,

can run as high as $300,000. Even taking inflation into account, that's a lot of zeros after the dollar sign. For the money, though, you are buying a true, real-people size, five-place-with-baggage airplane with a comfortable cabin; it will climb above most all the weather and cruise for 1,000 miles to boot. Not much else on the market can give this kind of performance at the same price.

Speaking of price, if the last four or five years are any indication of where the market for airplanes is heading, the chances are bet-

A pressurized Centurion landing. The windows are smaller than on the unpressurized model.

but not all. Lord, it swayed back and forth six inches when the mechanics cycled the gear.

After all was counted, those three switches cost $1,400 to replace—one of the reasons that the O-2A now resides in another hangar 2,000 miles from here. Someone else gets to play warbird owner while I stick to writing books.

Enough about money. If you're reading this chapter with the intention of buying a 210, then you have already figured out how much airplane you can afford without my somewhat biased advice.

Actually, my time behind the yoke of a Centurion has been very pleasant. My logbook shows that almost all of it was for plea-

sure trips to California and Nevada. I remember flying into Lake Tahoe Airport in Nevada (which means climbing over the Sierra Nevada mountains and onto an airstrip perched at 6,264ft) on a beautiful, 80-degree day. The trip gave me a great feeling of confidence in the 210's ability to perform with a load at altitude.

Usually when going over the Sierras, I like to have lots of air between me and the pointy stuff below. Sometimes this can lead to a problem that is somewhat common on turbocharged airplanes such as the T-210. Here you are, flying along at 12,500ft on your way to an airport whose elevation is 6,000ft below you and not very far in front. The ter-

The pressurized 210 has both cowl flaps and intercooler exhaust, easily seen on the nose. The early 210s had gear doors, but after numerous problems, they were modified to the configuration visible here.

rain around Lake Tahoe makes it easy to find yourself ten miles out and way too high. The options are to pull the power too far back and risk shock cooling the engine, or to try to be the first person to land a 210 at 200mph.

Not easy to do! Better that a little planning goes into the arrival.

Careful planning of the entire flight is of prime importance when flying an airplane with the speed capabilities of the 210. When you're drilling through the sky in your trusty 172 at 100kt, you have the luxury of laying out your cross-country flight without having to worry too much about your descent too far away from the airport. When you move up to a true 160kt airplane, however, you have to plan more than one waypoint at a time. Many a cracked cylinder has resulted from pulling the power back too fast on a turbocharged engine while trying to lose a lot of altitude in a short time. The 210 is an airplane that must be flown with a lot of skill.

If you have been accustomed to flying planes in the Cessna 172/Piper Archer class, you should get a minimum of 5 hours of in-struction and a high-performance checkout before lighting off a 210. Probably your insur-ance company will require quite a bit more than just a few hours dual and 200 hours in the old logbook before it will want to issue coverage. Last time I checked with AVEM-CO, they were talking about 15 hours of in-struction and 250 hours of retractable time before they would quote a reasonable price for insurance. If you are looking at a pressur-ized P-210, figure on a 40 percent bump in rates. A sample quote for a private pilot with 500 hours of retractable time and 1,500 hours in the logbook was around $5,500 per year for a 1984 210 with a hull value of $165,000. And he got that price after much shopping around for the best rates. The insurance bro-ker told him that when a pilot's total time is under 500 hours with less than 25 hours re-tractable, they wouldn't issue any coverage, regardless of cost. It pays to have logged 1,000 hours before stepping into a 210.

When looking at an older 210, check the logbook before you even open the door. Re-member the number one rule: No logs, no sale. That is, unless you are interested in spending lots of money trying to restore a twenty-year-old airplane of unknown ances-try and dubious condition.

There are a few ADs that crop up on the 210 that can be very expensive. One of the older ADs that has to be checked covers prop overhaul on the early models of the 210. If the overhaul isn't done before you buy the plane, you could be surprised with a $3,500 bill be-fore it leaves the ground. Also, any older air-plane will have developed its own particular problems. You should be prepared to spend money on little, interesting things that appear after purchase. Without a doubt, having a competent shop look over the airplane prior to its changing hands is a necessity.

One of the better ideas I've seen has been to ask the owner if he will pay for the neces-sary repairs if you pay for a fresh annual at time of purchase. This way anything major is covered, and the airplane starts out with a new annual in the books.

What I have tried to do on any pur-chase is to work with the shop doing the in-spection. This way I can save some money by pulling the jillions of screws that hold all the covers and plates. Also, I get to know the airplane by doing some of the work my-self.

However, if you're the kind who doesn't know which end of the screwdriver to ham-mer with, then using a shop you trust will be necessary when you get into a complicated, high-performance airplane.

All this shouldn't cause you to steer away from owning a 210. Any go-fast air-plane will take more to make it fly than its slower brethren. But the pleasure derived from flying a Centurion far outweighs the cost.

Having an airplane that can cover most of the United States with one or two fuel stops really opens up the world. Being able to fly from San Francisco to Seattle without hav-ing to plan an intermediate stop turns an all-day affair into a three-and-one-half-hour trip. And climbing above the rain and clouds in a pressurized single, with the distance measur-ing equipment (DME) indicating 165kt, is truly flying. All at once, a lot of destinations open up to weekend trips. After all, one of the biggest reasons to get in a 210 is to cover ground fast.

Arriving in style doesn't hurt either.

C-210 Rating
Investment: #2
Utility: #3
Popularity: #2

Cessna 208 Caravan

In front of me I have a Cessna Caravan Standard Order Form for aircraft manufac-tured in 1992. This is what you peruse when ordering a new airplane—something I've not had the pleasure of doing. Boy, I can dream, though.

The order form begins with a Caravan weighing in at 3,896lb empty. The first piece of equipment on the Standard List is "Basic Avionics Kit." This covers all the equipment necessary to talk to anyone with whom you might wish to pass the time of day. Or fly an IFR flight. I was going to count all the basic standard bits and surprise you with my

You really can't picture the size of the Cessna 208 Caravan without some familiar reference. Look at the size of the pilots in the cockpit. *Cessna Aircraft Company*

mathematical ability to count, but I have a low threshold for boredom; there are a whole lot of parts and things and switches that go on a standard Caravan. For instance, there's a "Ground Service Plug Receptacle." Kinky or what?

Then we flip over the page to "Optional Caravan Equipment." My, now I see where the money goes. First item is a "Silver Crown IFR Package." $19,490. This gives you marker beacons, King KX-165 nav-com glideslope, dual nav indicators, ADF, DME, transponder, and an encoding altimeter (a three-pointer).

Ummm, my first airplane cost less than this radio pack, and it flew. Air conditioning is offered as an option that weighs 165lb and costs $11,775; better want cool air real bad. Moving along, we find listed under "Utility Seating" an option for a "Relief Tube." It is item 69Q/R and costs a measly $410. If you've ever been on a long cross-country flight with airports very few and far between, you would think option 69Q/R would be listed as standard equipment.

Enough of making funny with Cessna's answer to a white freightliner that flies. I thing it's a pretty good airplane for hauling anything that fits through the doors or under the airplane in an optional ($26,130) cargo pod. Federal Express thinks the Caravan is slicker than a box of wet chickens—it's been Cessna's best customer when it comes to snapping up Caravans.

For those of you who have never stood under the wing of a Cessna 208 Caravan (to give it its full name), from a distance it looks kinda like a 206 or 207. You have to walk up to it and stare it straight in the door handle to get a good idea of how big an airplane it really is.

It carries a cargo that weighs as much as two Cessna 152s. The Grand Caravan goes even further, packing another 500lb into a fuselage four feet longer than a standard Caravan.

You can also get one of these flying pickup trucks up on a set of amphibious floats that lift the 208 up to 18.2ft, guaranteed to give an amphib Cub an inferiority complex. It is a large box with a turbine engine hung on the front.

Bush pilots have been known to fall over in fits of ecstasy when shown the Caravan amphibian. Think of being able to pack up to ten people and all their hunting or fishing gear into one airplane and fly 300 miles to a hidden, cobalt blue lake high in a wilderness mountain range. Sign me up!

The Grand Caravan really stretches things a bit. Wonder what the passenger did to make the pilots put him all by himself in the back? *Cessna Aircraft Company*

C-208 Specifications

Engine: Pratt & Whitney PT6A-114A of 675hp
Maximum Weight: 8,000lb takeoff, 7,800lb landing
Maximum Cruise: 184kt at 10,000ft
Range: 1,085nm at 10,000ft
Fuel Capacity: 335.6gal
Rate of Climb: 1,050fpm
Service Ceiling: 25,500ft
Takeoff Performance: 1,205ft ground roll; 2,210ft over 50ft obstacle
Landing Performance: 745ft ground roll; 1,655ft over 50ft obstacle
Stall Speed: 61kt
Standard Empty Weight: 3,810lb
Maximum Useful Load: 4,185lb
Wingspan: 52.1ft
Length: 37.6ft
Height: 14.8ft

Cessna also opened up the cargo door and shook everything except the pilot's seat out of a Grand Caravan and called the remaining empty aluminum tube a Super Cargomaster. Picture a 340cu-ft box that flies at 175kt, and you'll have a good idea what it looks like.

One of the best Caravan tricks is going from a fourteen-passenger transport to an empty box full of boxes in a short time. It takes but a few hours to pull seats, unhook belts, remove carpeting (an option for $1,490), and start hauling large, bulky items.

What to look for when hunting a Cessna Caravan? Well, the first thing to do would be to find a Cessna Caravan. They aren't quite as common as, say, your average Cessna 182. A quick check through *Trade-A-Plane* only shows five different people selling 208s. And it looks like all of them are holding a good percent of their original price. Like 104 percent of new. Not too many bargains floating around. Probably none. Probably all the people who purchased a Caravan of one model or another are planning to keep it well into the twenty-fifth century or longer.

My advice for would-be, used Caravan buyers: look real hard at a new one. I know they cost over a mil and a half, but the oldest used one I could find was a 1986 with a 4,900 total time airframe (TTAF), 900 SMOH, full IFR, known ice, and ten seats. Set you back between $650,000 to $725,000 just for openers. That's half the price of a new Caravan, but with almost 5,000 hours on it. And those were real working hours, I would imagine. That plane would need something when you got it home. All used airplanes need something exactly ten minutes after your name is on the registration.

The cheapest Caravan I ever ran across was a 1984 Caravan I with high-time everything. The owner still wanted more than a half-million for it. Might have come down a couple thou . . . not real sure.

C-208 Rating
Investment: #2
Utility: #1
Popularity: #2 (Too big to be as popular as a 182, but close.)

Chapter 5

The Light Twins

Cessna 337 Skymaster

The Cessna 337 Skymaster was a try by Cessna to build a twin-engined airplane that could be flown by a pilot with a single-engine rating. It had one engine in front and one hung on the back, between twin booms. The idea was that if an engine decided to call it a day, the other could fly the airplane without the pull to one side caused by the drag of a dead engine. The loss of one engine would just make the airplane slow down, with little loss of control.

Well, the FAA, in its wisdom, said there was no way it would consider the 337 a single with a little more oomph stuck on the back. The best they would go for was a multi-engine centerline thrust rating. This meant you could fly the twin-engined 337,

A Turbo Skymaster II arrives. The plastic rectangle on the pilot's windshield is for deice.

C-337 Specifications

Engines:
C-337—Continental IO-360-C of 210hp with 1,500-hour TBO
T-337—Continental TSIO-360-A of 210hp with 1,400-hour TBO
Maximum Weight:
Super Skymaster—4,300lb
Skymaster—3,900lb
O-2A with pylons and miniguns—5,000lb
Fuel Capacity, Standard: 93gal
Fuel Capacity, Optional: 131gal
Maximum Cruise:
C-337—192mph
T-337—221mph
P-337—243mph at 20,000ft
Range (No Reserve): 765 miles, 4.0 hours with 92gal usable fuel
Range (No Reserve): 1,070 miles, 5.6 hours with 128gal usable fuel
Rate of Climb, Both Engines: 1,250fpm
Rate of Climb, Front Engine Only: 335fpm
Rate of Climb, Rear Engine Only: 415fpm
Service Ceiling, Both Engines: 20,000ft
Service Ceiling, Front Engine Only: 7,500ft
Service Ceiling, Rear Engine Only: 9,500ft
Takeoff: 845ft ground roll; 1,490ft over 50ft obstacle
Stall Speed with Flaps Down, Power Off: 66mph
Empty Weight: 2,615lb
Maximum Useful Load: 1,685lb
Wing Span: 38ft
Length: 29ft, 9in
Height: 9ft, 4in

but you couldn't go play with the rest of the twins.

Actually, Cessna had a pretty good idea with the push-pull concept. Not only did it make for a safer way to have a twin, but with the high wing configuration, it also gave better visibility than that from most other multis. The US Air Force agreed with Cessna to the point of converting the 337 to the O-2A (Observation, Second Type, First Model) and the O-2B, both of which got their wheels flown off during the Vietnam War. The Air Force continued to use the two up into the nineties as spotter aircraft for bombing ranges. It's not unusual to find an O-2A with over 6,000 hours on the airframe and a few patches where it was hit by small arms fire while playing in Southeast Asia.

Cessna actually built the Skymaster as a fixed-gear aircraft, called the 336. But this version is quite rare today. It was last built in 1964. I guess Cessna tried to build a twin that a pilot could move into from a 172 without having to learn about a gear lever. Without going very fast either, as the 336's gear hanging in the breeze caused it to be 10–15mph slower than the 337.

Actual transition into a 337 from a fixed-gear single was not much of a problem. You had to be aware that it was about 1,000lb heavier than what you were used to. When the power was turned off, the houses got bigger, faster. It definitely wasn't a 182 with another motor hung off the back. However, after fifty or so hours with the Skymaster, the 172 felt like a little airplane. Having had 420hp to play with, going back to 160hp felt like you were painted on the runway.

Once you get comfortable flying with two sets of engine and propeller controls, the Skymaster becomes a rather pleasant way to cover ground. At first there seems to be an awful lot to do for just having one propeller in front of you. It takes a bit of time to figure out how to get the props synchronized, as in any multi-engine. After the first couple of hours trying to learn what to push how far and connected to what with a lot of gauges to watch, everything gets easier. In fact, flying the Skymaster gets to be a lot of fun.

I must say that the first time the instructor pulls the power and feathers the front prop to a standstill will be a very strange sensation. The 337 slows down a bit, you add a little up trim, and you fly along with the prop staring you in the face. If you move up from a 182 or a 210, this will definitely provoke some strange feelings.

One thing that you have to watch very carefully in the Skymaster is engine temperature. Both engines depend on cowl flaps for additional cooling when on the ground or during climb-out. On a hot day, say over 85 degrees, the rear engine can pick up a lot of heat in a hurry. The best way to manage engine temperature is to watch the oil temperature, oil pressure, and cylinder head temperature closely. Even if one of the gauges isn't quite accurate, you can tell what's going on by watching the relationship of all three. If the oil temp starts to climb high in the green, the oil pressure will drop accordingly. The cylinder head temperature will climb with the oil temperature, but sometimes it lags behind on a hot, heavy climb. Keeping the cowl flaps open enough to run in the middle of the green and letting the engines run a little rich is not the fastest nor the most economical way to cover ground; but at last look, an IO-360 Continental was running about $12,000 to replace—and there are two of them. Others may differ with my methods. That's OK; I'm the one who has to replace cooked cylinders. Most of the Skymaster people I talked to ran the same way as far as dealing with heat. It makes more sense to me that running in the

middle ranges of the green on the gauges for an air-cooled engine will make for a longer life.

The usual cautions about reading the logs especially apply to the Skymaster, as well as to any multi. It may not be true that two engines mean four times the cost, but according to my checkbook it seems pretty close. When the airplane goes in for an oil change, a minimum of sixteen to twenty quarts hit the drain pan. The reason I say sixteen to twenty is that my 337 didn't really like having ten quarts in each engine. In the first 10 hours after an oil change, it blew black glop all down the underside and all over the rear prop and elevator until it got the oil level down around eight quarts. Then it happily chugged along for hours without throwing

A close-up of the intercooler scoop on the front engine of a T-337. Airflow through the scoop provides cooling for the intake air compressed by the turbocharger, lowering the combustion inlet air temperature.

The 337's main gear doors. The gear retracts backwards into the fuselage. Inside the gear bay showing some of the hoses and fittings used to retract the landing gear.

any oil to speak of. Some oil always found its way out of each engine, no matter what was replaced or tightened. The mechanic who kept all the parts going in the same direction must have owned English cars. He said the only time these engines quit leaking is when they're out of oil.

Hang a turbocharger on each engine and pressurize the fuselage, and the 337 begins to really perform up high in the Flight Level (FL) 210 area. It will carry an 800lb load, after fueling, up at 20,000ft for 900 miles with speeds in the 225mph range. It can get off the ground in a 900ft roll at maximum gross

The front office of a turbo 337 contains a lot of things to push, pull and turn. It's actually harder than it looks.

Cessna offered an optional cargo pad for some of its singles. Here's one installed on a Skymaster.

Looks awkward but the flying qualities of the airplane are unchanged.

weight. If you keep up your end of the bargain, the turbo 337 will come to a halt using 600ft of runway. Now, if you are the one buying the brake pads, you might want to let it roll a little farther before clamping on the binders.

Nice to know that it will stop in less than 1,000ft if you need it to, though. Like when, through a bad case of brain fade, I ended up not touching down until most of the runway had vanished behind me. I managed to come to in time to get stopped with some runway left in front of the nose wheel (at least 12ft); should have gone around. I didn't match the factory pilot's 590ft stop, though I dropped it in with full flaps and the stall horn playing melodies in my ear; used up less than 800ft to a full stop. No, the brakes didn't fade. Just took a while to cool down to where you could touch the tires. Won't do that again anytime soon.

Jack Riley, owner of Riley Aircraft, takes a late model Skymaster apart to the bare metal, remanufactures everything, fills the panel with everything except color TV (but you might ask), installs the finest interior seen in airplanes, and generally builds an extra-deluxe pressurized 337 called the Riley Rocket. The Rockets are very nice airplanes, faster than stock by a good margin. They tend to be a bit pricey. Up around the half-million mark for a fresh conversion, last I looked. If you want the ultimate in twin, centerline thrust, and if you want speeds in the 250mph range and like the look of leather in a perfect interior, go for one. When you get it, I possibly could be talked into a ride.

This is what you look for when 310 shopping. Low-time engines and props, almost new King Silver Crown radios and fresh paint.

Now, what kind of expense would you be looking at for, say, a good 1974 to 1978 Skymaster, no turbos, good panel, low-time engines and props?

I found a 1974 C-337G with 1,650 TT, fewer than 500 hours on both engines, good King radios, a Robertson short takeoff and landing (STOL) kit, an intercom, and six seats, for an asking price of $65,000. According to the Blue Book, this is on the high side, so I'd want to see how the airplane showed. I'd let an FBO have a good look before the money changed hands.

If you want an average 1967 to 1971 337 to go chug around the sky, the mid-twenties will buy a lot of airplanes. You know how I feel about the 337, so anything in this book probably is bent in a positive direction. I think centerline thrust for a low horsepower twin (under 275hp) makes a lot of sense. The biggest reason for a light twin over a high-pop single, such as an A-36 Bonanza, is the safety of the second engine. But most people who buy light twins, other than FBOs for

This is what it looks like when both engines on a 310 have to be rebuilt, an expensive sight. If everything from the firewall forward is remanufactured, expect to see a bill of $20,000 per side.

training, don't have a whole lot of time in complex airplanes, and for inexperienced pilots, a twin with one engine out is potentially more dangerous than a single with its engine out. I think statistics will bear me out when I say that those low-time pilots who lose an engine in a conventional twin stand a better chance of arriving at the ground in an unplanned position than someone who loses an engine in a single. An engine loss in a 337 is a fairly anticlimactic affair. One prop stops turning, and you go find a place to land. No massive amounts of opposite rudder, no possibility of turning into a dead engine, with a stall-spin as the reward for doing it wrong. I'll gladly listen to other voices, but I lean heavily towards the 337 Skymaster in all its forms.

C-337 Rating
Investment: #4
Utility: #2
Popularity: #4

Cessna 310

The Cessna 310 was built from 1955 to 1981. A total of almost 5,500 were produced. The aircraft picked up a weight increase of

A detail shot of a 310, showing the wide cockpit and rear window to good effect. The new polyurethane paint looks about two feet deep.

900lb from its original 4,600lb gross weight. Engine horsepower went from 480 total to 570 total over its twenty-six-year life, with a resultant speed gain of 47kt from the first 310's 190kt. Service ceiling with the turbo engines is 27,400ft, with a 17,200ft limit for single-engine operation.

Well, if it was good enough for Sky King to fly, I guess the Cessna 310 is OK for you or me to fly. In the original TV series Sky King, Sky's second airplane (named Song Bird II) was a 1958 C-310B. His third aircraft, Song Bird III, was a 1960 C-310D. Probably the two most recognizable aircraft on television.

After a bit, even the military got into the picture. The US Air Force opted for thirty-five C-310s, calling them U-3Bs. They flew with a weight increase of 160lb over the 1960 version's gross weight of 4,830lb. If you are in the market for a 310 that could also double as a warbird at air shows, one of these might be

the way to go. I'd expect a real U-3B to be fairly hard to locate, as only thirty-five were built. Checking back through a few issues of *Trade-A-Plane*, I didn't find any. Did find a T-42 Cochise (military Beech Baron) in army colors with an asking price of $70,000, so I would figure a good U-3B to be in the same price range.

As with most other Cessnas, the price range for the 310 runs all over the page. A 1957 310B, with 4,189 TT and 1,179 on the engines, lots of new overhauled parts, but old radios, is listed for $24,900. The ad says "must sell," so what you would spend depends on how well you play poker.

A 310R, advertised as the most beautiful and best equipped one currently flying, with 2,690 TT, engines around 1,000 hours on factory rebuilds, and enough avionics to equip two other 310s, is marketing for $120,000. No year is specified, but it's right in the middle price range for C-310R models built from 1975 to the last year of manufacture, 1981.

Riley Aircraft Company took the Cessna 310 and remanufactured it in two versions, the Riley Rocket and the Riley Turbo Rocket. Riley completely stripped the airframes, installed custom interiors, repainted the airplanes, and improved the performance by hanging larger engines on the wings. These aircraft were manufactured in small numbers at a substantial cost increase over the standard 310, so be prepared to pay a healthy premium if you find one for sale.

The Cessna 320 Skyknight (Cessna's marketing department sure reached for those names) is a variant on the standard 310. It first appeared in 1962 as a slightly larger 310, with seating for up to seven and two Continental 260hp engines.

The 320's last model year was 1968, when it was called the Executive Skyknight 320-F. By then the engines had grown to 285hp.

Some of the 320s have been converted to use larger engines by RAM Aircraft Corp. of Waco, Texas. This modification bumps the speed up to 280mph by using the "more cubic inches = more go" theory of modification.

Preflighting a 310 before a cross country to Las Vegas from San Jose. The wing-to-fuselage fairing must make a smooth transition or a lot of drag and turbulence will result. Aircraft manufacturers work hard to make this juncture as smooth as possible.

One of the RAM conversions is currently advertised as "the best there is." It has a STOL kit, color radar, stormscope, full deice, loran and HSI, full autopilot, intercom, and much else. The asking price of $92,000 is way over the high Blue Book figure of $74,000. However, a lot of the asking price covers all the engine modifications and updated avionics. This one would have to be judged all by itself rather than simply compared to the average 320.

In another ad, the owner wants $25,000 firm for a high-time 1966 320 with both engines at or beyond TBO. From the photo in the ad, it appears that the airplane spent lots of time with people taking pictures through a 17x26in camera hole in the belly. Figure two Continental engines and two prop remanufactures will set you back about $37,000 to $42,000 if nothing else pops up on rebuild.

The total price for the 320 with new engines and props would be in the $65,000 range when all was said and done. For that much money, you could buy a nice, low-time 310 or 320, with mid-time or lower engines, already flying.

Weather radar and loran dominate the 310's panel. Some of the rest of the avionics look to have been stuck wherever they would fit; this is always a problem when trying to upgrade or add newer equipment to an older panel. To rip everything out and build a modern avionics center stack is prohibitively expensive. This 310H is a 1963 model in good condition after thirty years of use.

After years of use and minutes of care, this 310 nacelle shows its age. When looking at a used airplane, check the rivet heads around the engine for oil trails as under the spinner on this engine. This is a good way to find hidden oil leaks.

If you want a light twin and want to keep it into the next century, buying a cheaper airplane with runout engines and building it back as you want it probably would be the way to go.

Of course, if you have the same mechanical aptitude and drive as I do (read: none), then a low-time 310 or 320, for more money initially, will prove to be the best investment in the long run.

Buy a 310 and maybe you can star in your own TV show.

C-310 Rating
Investment: #4
Utility: #3
Popularity: #3

Cessna 335 and 340

The Cessna 335 and 340 are virtually the same airplane with one major difference: the 340 is pressurized. One requires oxygen masks to go high; the other pumps up the whole cabin. And you're right if you are thinking that blowing up the fuselage every time you go for a ride will cost more money in maintenance. There's a pretty good chunk of change difference between the value of the two airplanes, also. An average 1980 C-335 will run about $130,000, while a C-340 of the same vintage will lighten the wallet by $194,000. Quite a difference between wearing a mask or not. However, if you own the airplane as a business craft that spends most of its time hauling people who are unfamiliar with airplanes over trips of 200–500 miles, the time difference between the two is only five minutes, but the comfort level would be quite different. Business passengers really don't like to have to put on a nose bag to go for an airplane ride.

Although both the C-335 and C-340 are turbocharged, the C-335 usually spends most of its time making short hauls while running at altitudes below 10,000ft. The C-340 is more happy operating at the higher altitudes, where pressurization and turbocharging can be put to good use.

The C-340 was built from 1972 to 1984, while the C-335 appeared in 1980 and was gone by 1980. The C-335 was not a big seller.

C-335 and C-340 Specifications:
Engines, C-335: Continental TSIO-520-EB of 300hp with 1,400-hour TBO
Engines, C-340: Continental TSIO-520-NB 310hp with 1,400-hour TBO
Maximum Weight: 6,025lb
Fuel Capacity, Standard: 102gal
Fuel Capacity, Optional: 143gal, 166gal, or 207gal
Maximum Cruise, C-335: 195kt at 73.7% power and 10,000ft
Maximum Cruise, C-340: 229kt at 74.8% power and 24,500ft
Range: 372–1,377nm
Rate of Climb, C-335: 1,400fpm; 200fpm single engine
Rate of Climb, C-340 1,650fpm; 315fpm single engine
Service Ceiling, C-335: 28,600ft; 11,500ft single engine
Service Ceiling, C-340: 29,800ft; 15,800ft single engine
Takeoff Performance, C-335: 1,850ft ground roll; 2,365ft over 50ft obstacle
Takeoff Performance, C-340: 1,615ft ground roll; 2,175ft over 50ft obstacle
Landing Performance: 770ft ground roll; 1,850ft over 50ft obstacle
Stall Speed: 71kt
Standard Empty Weight, C-335: 3,749lb
Standard Empty Weight, C-340: 3,911lb
Maximum Useful Load, C-335: 2,276lb
Maximum Useful Load, C-340: 2,114lb
Wing Span: 38ft, 1.3in
Length: 34ft, 4in
Height: 12ft, 7in

Cessna stuck with the 340 for thirteen years, having developed it from the C-320 as a six-passenger, pressurized, light twin that could operate in comfort at altitudes up to 23,000ft. For the small company with short hauls and three to six people going along for the ride, the C-340 makes much sense. Also, it's the cheapest way to fly six people for 500 miles with the pressure turned on.

As with a lot of the other light twins floating around, RAM has made a higher horsepower version of the 340 with 335hp engines, intercoolers, and updated avionics. The RAM conversion of the 340 seems to be holding around $230,000 for a 1979 to 1981 model. A standard C-340, without de-ice capabilities or radar, brings around $130,000. That's a wide span of prices between high and low, but looking at the two aircraft, it is easy to see where the $100,000 is hiding. Again, you get what you pay for, with a few surprises thrown in to keep up the interest quotient.

C-335 and C-340 Rating
Investment: #4
Utility: #4
Popularity: #3

Four businessmen departing for a meeting in their 1962 Cessna 310. *Cessna Aircraft Company*

Chapter 6

The Big Twins

Cessna 401 and 402 Business

Starting back in 1964, Cessna began building the first of the 400-series aircraft with the 411. The 401 and 402 showed up in 1967, both with Continental 300hp engines. As the years went on, the basic airplane got heavier, with more horsepower, different windows, and more avionics. Still the 400's original purpose remained—to act as an economical, low frills airplane that feeder airlines could use to economically haul six or seven passengers at 200mph to airports not served by the major air carriers.

By 1980, the 402 had grown from its initial gross weight of 6,300lb to 6,885lb maximum. Horsepower increased at the same time, from 300hp in the 1967 model to 325 for 1980. All the other specs took an increase along with the power and weight. Cessna was using its favorite trick of certifying a basic airframe, then pulling, pushing, and jumping up and down on it until it only loosely resembled the first concept.

By the time the 1980 C-402 arrived, the airplane had turned from a basic, medium-utility twin to a high-buck twin, loaded with all the modern conveniences that Cessna could pull off a drawing board.

The newer C-402s had a different window configuration, going from four rounded windows in 1970 to five rectangular windows on each side that tapered in size to the rear. Still the same 402 underneath.

The latest model, the 402C, is the best hauler in its class. It costs less than its competitors, costs less to fly, has the greatest range, and carries a 2,800lb load—300lb better than others in the same class.

The 402C gets off the ground in under 2,200ft, climbs at 1,450fpm, cruises at 194kt at 10,000ft, and can go to 26,000ft if warranted. It can haul ten commuters over a 200-mile trip cheaper than any other airplane in its class.

It was built as a Businessliner with seats or as a Utililiner (who makes up these names?) with nothing but an empty aluminum tube to haul cargo. You can run the props off a 402, running a charter service seven days a week. Then pull the seats and haul canceled checks all night. It acts like its own one-airplane fleet.

I know I begin to sound like a Cessna ad man when discussing the 402, but it does serve its purpose better than anything else in its class.

In scouting for this airplane, you'll find it in a wide spectrum of prices and conditions. They run anywhere from a low-pop 1969 402A, with high-time everything and medium looks, for $75,000 or offer; to RAM conversions for $265,000. It's really a matter of judging each plane individually, giving it a careful prepurchase inspection, and getting the opinion of someone who has a lot of experience looking inside a 401 or 402.

An unpressurized Cessna 411. The 411 is similar to the C-414 and 421A.

When looking at any airplane financed by a financial institution of one sort or another, it would behoove you to inform your lending agency about what you intend to do. With the current climate of recession and law-suit-crazed people wandering around airplanes, banks are getting very skittish about letting go of someone's hard-earned, recently deposited money for an airplane purchase, unless all the ducks are in a row. Money concerns and product liabilities are assuming greater importance every week. No one wants to wake up one morning to find

out they are being sued for $11 million because they installed a gyro horizon in an airplane fourteen years and six owners ago. As long as people are looking to place the blame for everything from a hangnail to a handgun on someone other than themselves, the situation with airplanes and financing won't get any better.

C-401 and C-402 Rating
Investment: #4
Utility: #1
Popularity: #2

Cessna 404 Titan

Just when you thought you had all the 401/402 models of Cessna all figured out, along comes the C-404 Titan. It's the largest of Cessna's unpressurized aircraft, built from 1976 to 1981. It was not real popular because, with 375hp, it was 60mph slower than the 425 Corsair it resembled. The 404 ran 230mph, compared to the turboprop 425's 290mph.

The Titan would haul more payload than a 402C by about 750lb. It burned the additional fuel on the trip also. An average trip of 500 miles would see the Titan haul more weight than the 402C at the same speed with a 30 percent higher fuel burn. No free lunch.

The Titan was almost as far as Cessna could go with the same basic 401 airframe and not have to put wider pages in its sales brochures. It was about three feet longer than the standard 402, with a wing that was two feet wider. It had a whole group more maximum gross weight than a 402C—8,450lb compared to 6,885lb.

The Titan is set up to carry up to a half ton of cargo outside the cabin. It has wing lockers and two nose lockers—lots of places to forget where you put your suitcase. With all the weight on board, the Titan will haul itself over the proverbial 50ft obstacle in a tad over 2,300ft, climb at 1,500fpm, and cruise at 180kt. If you turn the burner down to economy, you can carry a load of cargo, full fuel weight of one ton, and cover 1,840nm with reserves. This event would consume about eleven-and-a-half hours of your life, after which you would be a blithering idiot needing a new bladder. I don't know who, at Cessna, figures out these range and endurance profiles, but you can bet a new pair of shoes that he never sat in the plane to prove it could be done. I think the longest I was able to sit in a seat was some five-and-a-half hours in my Cessna O-2A going to an airshow a long, long ways away. However, the pilots who first took the O-2As to Vietnam left from Hamilton AFB near San Francisco and flew nonstop to Hickam Field in Hawaii. Groooaaan!

Anyway, 404 Titans run the price gamut from worn-out beaters for $220,000 to sparkling fresh rebuilds for $360,000. All of these planes had to go to work at an early age, with no respect for child labor laws, so expect to find that a low-time 404 means under 10,000 hours. Not much under either.

C-404 Rating
Investment: #4
Utility: #1
Popularity: #4

Aircraft Brokers

Conversation with Dan Jay of Lafferty Aircraft Sales, San Jose International Airport, about aircraft brokers.

"Unlike automobile ownership in the State of California where we have a "Pink Slip" of ownership, aircraft ownership is dictated by the way that they are registered by the FAA at Oklahoma City. It's a little more complicated process, so it helps to know who you're dealing with and have all the financing, be it a bank or someone who specializes in financing aircraft, set up in advance. Even the best laid out deals fall through. It can happen that when an individual takes an airplane to his friendly banker, the airplane is a strange entity. The banker doesn't understand the process by which aircraft change ownership.

"When buying a Cessna in the light twin or a Citation range, the primary advantage of dealing with a broker is that we have a better grasp of the quality of the aircraft in the marketplace, what's available at a given time. We do work both as the buyer's agent and the seller's agent. It's like real estate to a certain point, however, neither the buyer nor the seller is compromised by us playing the other role. Word of mouth amongst reputable dealers is very important.

"The dealer can cast a much wider net than an individual. The broker has much less chance of getting burned on a deal than an individual. If another broker doesn't disclose the actual condition of an airplane or has us make an unnecessary trip to inspect a misrepresented airplane, he knows it won't happen again. It happened to me just recently. I went back to Illinois to inspect an airplane and was very disgusted with the condition of the aircraft. We made it very clear that we wouldn't deal with him again. He knew our standards and he should have known better. I would say that anyone looking for an airplane in the twin or larger class, just about needs to deal through a broker in order to insure that he gets the best deal available, both in price and aircraft condition."

Behind each engine on the 411 is a baggage lock-er. Because of engine heat, it is not a good idea to put anything in there that will melt.

Cessna 411, 414, 421A, and 421B

These airplanes belong to a series of similar twins, all with tip tanks, long noses and four- or five-passenger windows. The model production began in 1965 with the unpressurized 411. In 1967 pressurized versions came along with the 421, a six- to eight-passenger twin. Later the 414 was added as a lower priced model of the 421. The last 421 Golden Eagle came down Cessna's assembly line in 1986. Powered by two Continental 375hp turbocharged engines, it has a gross weight of 7,500lb and will carry that along at 225mph over a 1,483nm range—if you can stand the airplane for almost 8 hours.

A more likely mission for the 411/421 series would be a 500nm flight in a 421, cruising at 25,000ft. Block-to-block time would be 2 hours 30min, with a speed of 223kt. It would burn slightly over 600lb of fuel to transport a 1,700lb payload.

The C-411 tops out at 6,500lb gross weight, with an empty weight of 3,865lb. Its mission profile would be a 200-mile flight at 65 percent power for a speed of 232mph.

The 414 pressurized twin was planned in 1969 as a step-up aircraft for owners of Cessna or other light twins. It uses the fuselage and tail of the 421, with the wing of the 402. Cessna playing mix and match again.

The 414 has a maximum gross weight of 6,750lb with a maximum useful load of 2,429lb. A typical flight would cover 500nm in 2:42 while cruising at 202kt at 25,000ft, burning 520lb of fuel.

Back when Cessna Finance was still writing paper on one of these twins, it was possible to outfit them in a multitude of options. Here again, most of the standard Cessna 300-or 400-series radios are now holding down shelves in the back rooms of avionics shops. Not that the ARC stuff was unreliable. It's just that Collins ProLine or King Silver Crown are so much better. Of course, most of these airplanes are equipped with state-of-the-art color radar, GPS, VLF/Omega, dual VSI, dual DME-40, dual PN-101 compass, Alt-50 radar altimeter, RMI, dual PC-15B inverters, KLN-88 King loran with coupled moving map, HF radio, altitude alert, Bendix M4D autopilot with 4in dual HSI and flight director, etc., etc., etc. Rather hard to get lost, one would think,

with all the whistles and bells in front of one's face. I wonder how many hours after getting out of flight training it takes before a pilot is totally familiar with everything in the panel?

Last, but hardly least: prices. It's easy to nail down a price for a 411, 414, or 421. Figure anywhere from $47,000 for a 1968 411 to $470,000 for a 1985 421 Golden Eagle. Easy, huh?

Again it comes to figuring out what types of missions the airplane will be flying, what kind of money you are willing to part with, and how much the hourly operating cost will be for the particular model you select. Good wishes and endless patience be upon you.

C-411, C-414, and C-421 Rating
Investment: #4 (Some still depreciating. You won't probably get all your investment back.)
Utility: #1 (They do earn a living.)
Popularity: #2

Tip tanks and portion of a deice boot on the right wing of a 411.

Cessna 421 Golden Eagle. Cessna made a number of medium twins very similar in appearance, all piston engine. This one is a pressurized, eight-passenger model that is used mostly on short commuter hauls.

Cessna 425 Corsair, 425 Conquest I, and 441 Conquest II

Cessna's answer to the kerosene crowd was to build two versions of the Conquest and, for a short two years (1981–1982), the Corsair.

Built since 1975, the 441 was temporarily decertified because the tail had the nasty habit of falling apart. All the problems were traced to metal fatigue in the tail plane. Since then, Cessna has redesigned the tail, with a lot of additional strengthening, cur-

ing all the problems with parts falling off.

The Conquest has a maximum weight of 9,925lb with a zero fuel weight of 8,500lb. The approximate empty weight depends to a great deal on how the airplane is optioned, usually running in the neighborhood of 5,700lb. It has a cruise at 16,000ft of 295kt at 100 percent rpm. At a more likely rpm of 96 percent, you can plan to see numbers like 293kt at 24,000ft.

The 441 will carry up to eleven 170lb people at altitude for 1,200nm. However,

The exhaust pipe is barely visible in this shot of the left engine nacelle on the 421. The pressurized 421 doesn't have an opening storm window on the pilot's side.

most missions would be with a crew of two flying six to eight passengers over a 800nm flight. With a full complement aboard, the 441 will get off the ground after a roll of 1,800ft. Landing will use 1,100ft on the ground, clearing the FAA's 50ft obstacle with a total of 1,875ft. It quits flying at 90kt with the gear and flaps up, 75 down and dirty. Fuel capacity is a total of 481.5gal, of which 475gal or 3,183lb is usable. Most flights don't carry full fuel if they are going to be of a 2–3-hour duration, preferring to trade fuel weight for revenue-generating cargo or passengers.

The Conquest is faster than commercial carriers on trips between places not normally served nonstop by them. Sometimes a trip on a commercial carrier (for example, from El Dorado, Arkansas, to St. Petersburg, Florida) will require a stop at a hub (in this case, Dallas) to connect with a flight to the destination airport. So a direct flight in a 441 can save as much as seven hours over the time required to fly on a major airline. The 441 will also provide a better work environment, making time in the air much more productive.

With a full fuel load, the 441 can airmail six people nonstop from Los Angeles to Washington D.C. For the business traveler, this means you can plan to go a long way in a short time, operating on your schedule rather than that of the airlines.

In addition to filling a niche that commercial carriers can't touch, the 441 is also touted by Cessna as its answer to small business jets. Again, that's because the Conquest can fly those six passengers on a long run nonstop, at less cost.

But Cessna also competes with itself, in a sense, with another new product. Like the turboprop Conquest, Cessna's turbofan CitationJet can now take a 1,200lb load a long way without a stop for fuel: 1,000nm, in fact—just 200nm less than the Conquest. And that's just 600lb less load than the Conquest will haul. This really doesn't complicate your choice of a plane, since the missions typically flown by the the Conquest

and the CitationJet differ quite a bit. The 441 is normally used to haul more people over fewer miles than the CitationJet—say 200nm to the jet's average of 500nm. For those short hops with heavy loads, the 441 is significantly more economical.

Actual cost for a 1985 C-441 Conquest versus a Citation I SP 501 of the same year will differ by up to $700,000, so purchase price has to be considered when deciding between a jet and a turboprop.

Going fishing in *Trade-A-Plane*, I reeled in a 1981 Conquest II, with 2,021 hours TT, available for $12,000 per month lease with additional money set aside for engine reserve. Since this airplane books for a tad over

The nose of the 421 is similar to the hose of the 411 in many ways. The 421 is able to operate above 30,000 feet at speeds of over 200 knots.

one million, the lease price seems fairly in line. The plane would cost more than that per month to own, assuming a down payment of twenty percent and a loan paid off over ten years. Payment on principal alone would be $8,330 per month without interest or money upfront figured in.

Older 441s don't exactly fall off the end of the earth when it comes to resale, either. The only 1978 Conquest I could dig up had an asking price in the $930,000 range, so they do hold value pretty well.

The Corsair and the Conquest I shared the model designation C-425. They were pressurized turboprop twins with six-to-eight seats, built on the C-421 Golden Eagle airframe. The 425 was billed as an affordable turboprop.

The C-441 Conquest II was first flown on September 12, 1978. It and its slightly revised brother the Conquest I were in production until 1986. In those eighteen years, Cessna had sales of 230 for the two combined.

The 425 has a gross weight of 8,275lb, 1,650lb lighter than its bigger 441 brother. The useful load is down by 925lb at 3,380lb. Cruise speed at 26,500ft with the whip laid on runs 250kt. If the horses don't have to work as hard, clopping along at economy cruise, 213kt will show for a range of 1,575nm in 7.5 hours.

Again, most flights are of a shorter duration, packing up to eight FAA people for a 780nm trip. (That's figured at an FAA average of 170lb, though that's since been upped. We getting bigger.) To go 1,400nm, you would be limited to four people and baggage at maximum cruise power.

The 425 has two Pratt &Whitney 450hp turbines providing motivation, while its bigger 441 brother mounts two Garrett 635hp turboprop engines. Just for your information, the Garrett TPE3318401 blower will run you around $150,000 when overhaul rolls around. Luckily this event happens only every 3,000 hours, so you have a long way to go. But other pleasantries pop up from time to time, such as hot-section inspections. So keep up that engine reserve. There are also a series of time-determined phase inspections due on the aircraft. If you are out Conquest hunting,

---

C-425 and C-441 Specifications

Engine, Conquest I: Pratt & Whitney PTA-112 of 450shp with 3500-hour TBO
Engine, Conquest II: Garrett TPE331-8-403S of 635.5shp with 3000-hour TBO
Maximum Weight, Conquest I: 8,275lb
Maximum Weight, Conquest II: 9,925lb
Fuel Capacity, Conquest I: 366gal
Fuel Capacity, Conquest II: 481.5gal
Maximum Cruise Speed, Conquest I: 250kt
Maximum Cruise Speed, Conquest II: 276kt
Range: 1,199–2,193nm
Rate of Climb, Conquest I: 2,027fpm; 434fpm single engine
Rate of Climb, Conquest II: 2,435fpm; 715fpm single engine
Service Ceiling, Conquest I: 34,700ft; 18,500ft single engine
Service Ceiling, Conquest II: 35,000ft; 21,380ft single engine
Takeoff Performance, Conquest I: 2,047ft ground roll; 2,341ft over 50ft obstacle
Takeoff Performance, Conquest II: 1,785ft ground roll; 2,465ft over 50ft obstacle
Landing Performance, Conquest I: 952ft ground roll; 2,145ft over 50ft obstacle
Landing Performance, Conquest II: 1,095ft ground roll; 1,875ft over 50ft obstacle
Stall Speed with Flaps Down, Conquest I: 79kt
Stall Speed with Flaps Up, Conquest I: 88kt
Stall Speed with Flaps Down, Conquest II: 75kt
Stall Speed with Flaps Up, Conquest II: 90kt
Standard Empty Weight, Conquest I: 4,846lb
Standard Empty Weight, Conquest II: 5,706lb
Max Useful Load, Conquest I: 3,429lb
Max Useful Load, Conquest II: 4,243lb
Wing Span, Conquest I: 44.12ft
Wing Span, Conquest II: 49.33ft
Length, Conquest I: 36.38ft
Length, Conquest II: 39.02ft
Height, Conquest I: 12.61ft
Height, Conquest II: 13.14ft

---

try to find one that has had all the phase inspections from II to VI done. Other than that, I would recommend that you work with an aircraft broker, a good FBO, and an honest bank when searching for a 441 or 425.

Conquest and Corsair Rating
Investment: #3
Utility: #1 (If they still fly, they still work for a living—unlike some writers.)
Popularity: #2 (High among the kerosene crowd.)

Chapter 7

The Warbirds

Rather than getting into a blow-by-blow description of Cessna's military arm in the last thirty years, we'll cover the warbirds individually. They are fairly rare, not often seen in the general aviation market.

At least I haven't seen advertised in *Trade-A-Plane:*

For Sale: Cessna A-37 (Dragonfly), new miniguns, all ordnance in compliance with N.A.T.O. specs, digital TACAN, all weapons systems operational, light battle damage. Contact Director of Surplus Equipment, Sandino Aeropuerto, Managua, Nicaragua (MGA).

Mostly what is up for sale in the war-

Cessna T-37 Trainer. Also designated the A-37 Dragonfly and used as a light attack aircraft. This one's holding down the ramp for the Air Force Reserve in Texas.

birds section are airframes, wings, and related parts that have spent some very hard hours making a living. Since most of these airplanes are still out playing war, the chance of finding one all put together and flying ranks right up there with autographs of the Loch Ness monster.

T-37 and A-37 Dragonfly

For those of you who haven't misspent your productive years trying to make an ex-military airplane fly, a short description of the A-37 Dragonfly and its sister ship, the T-37, is in order.

The A-37 is a two-place, side-by-side, counter-insurgency attack aircraft. It has two

A-37 and T-37B Specifications
Engines: Pratt & Whitney J-85 turbojets of 6,000lb thrust
Maximum Speed: 507mph (Mach 0.658 at sea level)
Maximum Range: 462nm on internal fuel
Length: 29.3ft
Wingspan: 33.5ft

General Electric turbines mounted in the fuselage for motivation and 4,900lb of rockets, bombs, and other unpleasant surprises mounted under the wings. Just in case the locals want to check its ID, it carries one

The office of the T-37, showing the ejection seats with their parachutes. The canopy raises on a single hydraulic ram behind the seats and is held shut with four latches along the bottom.

Because of the wide stance of the landing gear, the T-37 is very forgiving on the runway. You can clearly see the twin intakes for the two engines.

Many of these aircraft are still flying as front-line attack airplanes with some of the world's air forces.

7.62mm minigun in the nose as identification. Never has a problem crashing parties. Stands out on a ramp.

With the government buying the jet fuel, the A-37 motivates along at 475mph or more for 1,400mi. Two turbojets provide almost 6,000lb of thrust, which helps when you're hot and heavy, carrying a full weapons load.

This is probably not the airplane for someone trying to move up from a 182. If you are trying to teach air combat maneuvers, take over a third-world country, or own a real rare (read: expensive) Cessna warbird, it's just the thing to park in your hangar.

I probably wouldn't trade more than my title to my house, first-born child, or entire retirement to own one. I've talked to a few Air Force Reserve pilots at air shows, when they were parked next to my O-2A: they all say they have a hard time believing that someone will pay them to spend a weekend at an airshow, to answer questions and fly the bird.

I have heard of a few people, knee-deep into jet warbirds, who have managed to get

The instructor and his student are almost ready to go. Note the covers over the helmets' visors to keep them from getting scratched while not in use.

Judging by the wear and chipped paint, this T-37 has seen a lot of different hands on its yokes.

almost enough parts to make one T-37B trainer version of the Dragonfly flyable. Not many.

Well, if you don't think a $250,000 A-37 is on your shopping list, then maybe you're ready for a smaller Cessna warbird.

Rating A-37 and T-37B
Investment: #5 (It will cost a whole group to make one fly; more to keep it going.)
Utility: #5 (Unless you want to start a minor war.)
Popularity: #4

O-1 and L-19 Bird Dog

The O-1 was first built for the US Army to function as a light recon or observation airplane, along with hauling general officers, delivering mail, taking someone from where he wasn't needed to where he wasn't wanted, and packing the trash. The O-1 has the dubious distinction of being one of the last planes to be shot down in the Vietnam war, crashing in downtown Saigon. Bird Dogs were built from 1950 to 1962.

A single-engine taildragger, the Bird Dog packs a Continental up front and a tailwheel in the back and all the fun and games that go with having a narrow-track taildragger. It's actually a very nice airplane. As warbirds go, it's about as simple as a baseball bat and just about as indestructible. Some 3,400 of them have been built, rebuilt, and then rebuilt again. Many countries throughout the world still have at least one or two in their inventories. Parts are easy to locate. I was going to say "cheap" in front of the word "easy," but you know how it is with airplanes. Bring money!

A gaggle of the O-1s have gathered together as the International Bird Dog Association. You can reach them at the address listed in the appendix. Without a doubt, they are the definitive source for information on the O-1.

Prices seem to run all around the map, depending on who did what to what model, what year. A really clean version replete with military paint from some obscure country that you wouldn't even think had an air force, much less a Bird Dog, will run in the $40,000 area. One in numerous boxes with "almost all the parts needed to finish" will run you a whole lot more by the time it makes its first flight with you as the proud (but poorer) pilot.

Usually when someone buys a collection of boxes, purported to be most of an airplane,

A typical Cessna tail, a giveaway as to the manufacturer of the T-37. This tail is dragged through the air a lot faster than the tail on your average 172, cutting the air at a little over 500mph. A stall speed of under 100mph makes for a very stable weapons platform.

he finds out that the amount of work necessary to assemble and register something like the O-1 or any other small warbird (warbug?) is much greater than anticipated. Frequently by a factor of two or more. Unless you are very familiar with the specific type aircraft, whose parts you lust after, buy one that will at least fly on a ferry permit, if not one that is fully registered with the FAA.

O-1 and L-19 Bird Dog Rating
Investment: #3
Utility: #5
Popularity: #3

O-2A

The O-2A replaced the O-1 when the US Air Force saw that the O-1 really wasn't suitable for the state of combat at the time we entered the conflict in Southeast Asia. Though the O-1 had a single engine and the O-2A had two, the biggest difference between them was speed. The O-1 was slower, and thus more susceptible to small arms fire. What was needed was an airplane with more go, the survivability of two engines, and a cockpit that gave outstanding visibility. The 337 Skymaster was the only civilian airplane that could be turned into a FAC airplane in the

A Cessna O-2A forward air controller. Cessna supplied the Air Force with this military version of the Model 337. Note the window in front of the single door. With the pilot's seat forward of the wing, visibility was almost 360 degrees.

The interior of the O-2A was much changed from the civilian airplane. The switches mounted on the top panel control the rockets and miniguns. The gunsight is to the left of the rocket panel. The Air Force even provided the copilot with his own ashtray, to the right of the copilot's control yoke.

limited time allowed. So Cessna came up with the O-2A to replace its original O-1 observation aircraft.

The O-2A is the military designation of the Cessna civilian Model 337. It came off the assembly line at Cessna to become an Air Force FAC with a few, small changes. That's if you consider rocket pods, miniguns, and a full military panel, replete with gunsight, a few, small changes.

A few more than 500 Cessna O-2As and O-2Bs were built. Some 160 of them didn't make it home from battle.

The O-2B was not as converted to military specs as the O-2A. The B model was mostly used for psychological warfare. It had a large speaker mounted in the space normally filled with the cargo door. This high-wattage blaster was hooked to a tape deck mounted in the aft cockpit area. Also, a leaflet dispenser was mounted through the cabin deck.

The O-2B flew around Vietnam dropping flyers and generally making a lot of noise in a foreign language, hoping to get some of their guys to become some of our guys. (Sounds like a recent election campaign.)

Anyway, a lot of the O-2 series Cessnas have found their way back to the United

This shot shows the rear engine with the cowl flaps fully open. If one engine was shot out or failed for any reason, the O-2A would get the pilot home on the other without the problems of asymmetrical thrust that would occur on a conventional twin. Also, if the gear failed to deploy, the front prop could be stopped horizontally and the airplane landed with the rear engine operating because it was set high enough above the centerline that the prop tips wouldn't touch the ground with the gear up.

States over the past twenty years. A few never left the country at all, preferring to stay home making a living as range spotters.

All the O-2s that are on the market have literally "been through the wars." Most airframes have 5,000-plus hard hours on them. They can be found in almost any condition: Some have large quantities of corroded aluminum, held together by spider webs and stringers; others look as though they've just flown their second hour.

I put one together three years ago, had a lot of adventures, and dropped in on a lot of airshows. I guess I am a little biased towards the O-2A, but I'll try to hold it down to a dull roar. This aircraft, USAF serial number 67-21363, had spent almost 3,000 hours in combat in Vietnam. When new, it was flown,

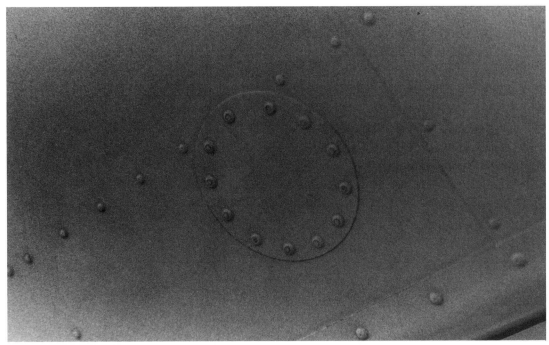

This is what a patch over a bullet hole in the wing looks like. The O-2A in the pictures flew over 3,000hr in Vietnam, acquiring nine of these patches in its career.

along with five others, from Hamilton Field, California, via Hawaii, Midway, and Wake Island to Nha Trang, Vietnam. There the O-2As were quickly stripped of all the ferry equipment and auxiliary fuel tanks—sometimes within the sound of battle—lit off, and flown into combat.

Mine evidently was one of the lucky ones, since it returned with only nine shrapnel or small arms holes in the airframe. One of the larger holes showed an entry down and behind the copilot's seat about 37mm in diameter, but no corresponding exit hole on the other side of the fuselage. From checking the records that came with the plane, we found that the pilot's plexiglass side window was replaced about halfway into the airplane's tour of duty. It's quite possible that the bullet entered the cockpit, missed both pilot and copilot, then exited through the left window, behind the pilot's head.

As I said, one of the lucky ones.

Right now, only a few of the civilian O-2s have come up for sale, so no market trend has developed. Probably the wisest course of action would be to latch onto someone who is restoring one around your area. Offer to help do some of the cleanup chores involved in restoring any warbird. After a while, the owner will probably put you to work on some of the easier jobs, guaranteeing sore arms and probably the cheapest education going. (No, I don't have my O-2A any more. But thanks for the offer.)

If you fancy arriving at an airshow with the whole family, three days worth of luggage, and two General Electric miniguns slung under the wings, then an O-2A might be the perfect airplane to own.

Expect to pay between $80,000 and $100,000 for a good one with low-time factory remanufactured engines, excellent paint, full military panel with gunsight, some civilian radios, and most of the bugs worked out. You don't have to worry about all the bugs being gone as the airplane will develop a

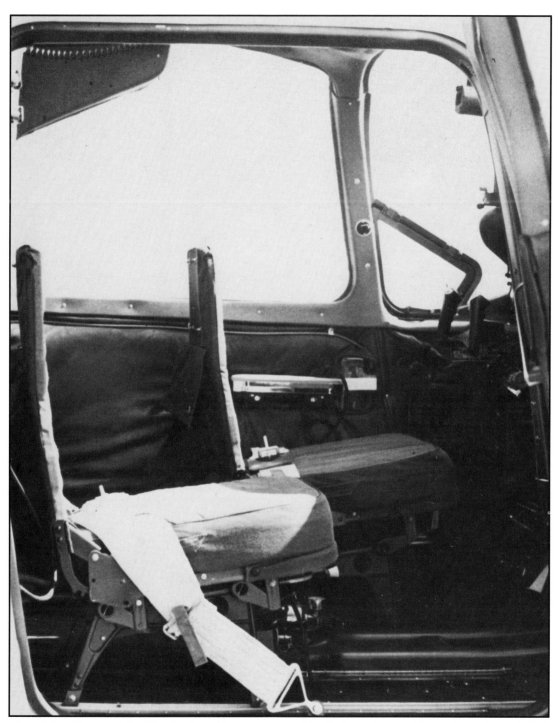

The seats of the O-2A had the back cushions removed so that the pilot could wear a parachute while flying. These seats are not the most comfortable of places to spend two or three hours. What doesn't show is the armor or "chicken plates" that fit under the seat.

A 1967 model O-2A going on patrol. The miniguns and the 2.75in rocket launchers are quite visible. With 700lb of rockets and guns, a hot-day takeoff could be quite interesting.

whole new set for you to play with as soon as the ink dries on the bill of sale. Talk to any warbird owner, they all say that their airplanes always need something repaired.

Wouldn't be any fun if it all worked all the time, would it?

Remember my O-2A?

Well, when I became the lucky owner, after having bought it sight unseen, imagine my surprise when I stripped off the protec-

tive covering applied by the Air Force when mothballing airplanes and opened the door to an empty cockpit! Real empty!

No seats, no radios, no gauges, not much of anything. To add insult to injury, in the process of de-milling the aircraft some careful soul had used a number six pry bar to remove the armament panel from the top of the glareshield. Then the same tool was lovingly applied to the gunsight. After all the parts were so carefully handled by the skilled minions of the government, everything that had been pried off was left on the floor of the cockpit with a fine coat of yellow paint, skillfully sprayed upon their surfaces. I guess that was what the military meant when they informed me that the airplane would be transferred to civilian hands in a "de-milled" state. The interior must have gone through its own war, down there in the Arizona desert at Davis-Monthan storage facility.

You want to hear the long sad tale about how much, how long, and how hard it was to get the O-2A up to San Jose? All right, all right, but it made for a good tale. I was going to name the O-2A after the words of the raven in Edgar Allen Poe's poem, Never-more, 'cause I ain't nevermore going to do it no more.

Don't get me wrong. Owning a Cessna warbird is truly a rewarding experience. We went to many airshows as display. I got to fly in a few also.

The high point in my flying career was at a naval air station where I flew some airshow VIPs around the pattern three or four times. What made it so outrageous was that the Blue Angels took to the skies less than one hour after I flew. Imagine 150,000 people who came to the airshow to see the Blues perform, watching me fly 200mph low-level passes 40ft off the runway.

Compared to the Blue Angels' F/A-18s, it probably looked like the O-2A was painted on the runway. But it flipped my ego into af-

Almost all the rockets expended, an O-2A returns to base. Note the lack of prop spinners. The Air Force pulled the props down every 100hr for inspection.

terburner, I flat guarantee you. More fun than $700. Do you think I didn't have a problem with helmet size when I taxied back to the tiedown in front of all those people and all their spiffy cameras?

Go buy a Cessna O-1 or O-2, and get involved in airshows, especially the military versions. After the first one, I guarantee you won't remember any of the money or time spent. Won't matter, either.

O-2A Rating
Investment: #4
Utility: #5 (Unless you want to play FAC for the guy with the A-37.)
Popularity: #3 (Well, I liked mine a bunch. So did the people at air shows.)

T-41 Mescalero

The T-41 Mescalero was just what the military wanted when it set out to buy a basic trainer. It was used as the first step in sorting out those who want to be military pilots and those who are going to be military pilots. Very large difference! Mostly, a T-41 is a C-172 with a 210hp engine and a military paint job. Some 864 T-41s finally ended up as trainers. The Air Force doesn't use them any more, having gone to kerosene burners for all phases of flight training, so all the T-41s are now in private hands or doing duty with the Civil Air Patrol or some such organization. Prices tend to run in the $30,000 range, with the occasional asking price in the low $40s. Anything said about the C-172 applies to the T-41 as well.

Rating T-41 MESCALERO
Investment: #3
Utility: #4 (Unless you're working with the T-37 & O-2A guys above as a trainer.)
Popularity: #2 (It is a 172, after all.)

Chapter 8

The Dusters

Cessna AGwagon, AGtruck and AGcarryall

Cessna decided to get into the bug-killing business in the mid-1960s. The company took a good look at what was on the market with the idea of building the best agricultural airplanes possible.

The first design to hit the market was the AGwagon, out flying under power poles in 1966. Horsepower in the first series was provided by the same engine used in the C-182. Later models had the choice of the original 230hp or up to a 300hp Continental. By the early seventies, Cessna's AG aircraft com-

Cessna added a belly tank and spraybars to a 185 and called it the AGcarryall. *Peter M. Bowers*

pletely dominated the market. This was before the arrival of 600-plus horsepower turbine dusters and boom-rigged helicopters.

If you think a career spent flying 20ft off the ground in a heavy, loud airplane filled with chemicals, dodging wires, and laying down straight lines of spray sounds like a good way to spend your life, a Cessna AG airplane is probably for you.

Personally I'd rather stand on the side of the road watching a duster play ballet over a field of alfalfa, but some of you are just plane crazy—think flying one of these things is pleasurable. It does look like a good way to really learn how to fly—build lots of hours close to the ground. Bet no one falls asleep in their first 500 hours pushing bug spray out the hopper.

Cessna did such a good job on the first AGwagon it built, that the subsequent year's productions only incorporated small changes. All the various models are built only slightly less structurally sound than a Greyhound bus. They have to be, considering how they work and the people who depend on them to pay the bills.

Just about everything that will fit in the hopper and pour through a straw has been carried by the AGwagon and its siblings. Operators fertilize the ground, drop the seeds, kill the weeds, remove the bugs, and even clear the ground with dusters.

Most agricultural aircraft are set up to spray at night as well as during the day. There are a couple of advantages in doing it this way. Usually the air is still at night, so you get a better dispersal, more efficient use of the chemicals. Bugs tend to stay on the ground at night, not being certified for IFR or after-dark flying, allowing a better chance at control. And the pilot's brains don't broil so badly after the sun has disappeared, making the flying easier. Now operators hang large candlepower lights on the airplanes and station people at the field boundaries with more illumination to give the pilot almost all the vision of daylight flying. Not quite as easy as flying a Cessna Caravan full of canceled checks between cities at 3:00

AGwagon and AGtruck Specifications

Engine, 1976: Continental IO-520-D of 300hp with 1,700-hour TBO

Maximum Weight, 1976 AGwagon: 3,300lb, normal category; 4,000lb, restricted category

Maximum Weight, 1976 AGtruck: 3,300lb, normal category; 4,200lb, restricted category

Fuel Capacity, Standard: 37gal

Fuel Capacity, Optional: 54gal

Maximum Cruise: 140mph; 113mph with dispersal equipment

Range: 230 miles, 1.7 hours with 37gal usable fuel at 6,500ft

Rate of Climb: 940fpm; 690fpm with dispersal equipment

Service Ceiling: 15,700ft; 11,100ft with dispersal equipment

Takeoff Performance: 610ft ground roll; 970ft over 50ft obstacle

Landing Performance: 420ft ground roll; 1,265ft over 50ft obstacle

Stall Speed with Flaps Down, Power Off: 57mph

Standard Empty Weight, AGwagon: 1,985lb; 2,140lb with equipment

Standard Empty Weight, AGtruck: 2,059lb; 2,214lb with equipment

Hopper Capacity, AGwagon: 200gal

Hopper Capacity, AGtruck: 280gal

Wing Span, AGwagon: 40ft, 8.5in

Wing Span, AGtruck 41ft, 8in

Length: 26ft, 3in

Height: 8ft

Cessna AGcarryall Specifications

Engine, 1976: Continental IO-520-D of 300hp with 1,700-hour TBO

Maximum Weight, 1976: 3,350lb

Fuel Capacity, Standard: 61gal

Fuel Capacity, Optional: 80gal

Maximum Cruise: 140mph at 75% power and 7,500ft

Range: 395 miles, 2.9 hours with 55gal usable fuel at 7,500ft

Rate of Climb: 845fpm

Service Ceiling: 13,400ft

Takeoff Performance: 885ft ground roll; 1,450ft over 50ft obstacle

Landing Performance: 480ft ground roll; 1,400ft over 50ft obstacle

Stall Speed with Flaps Down, Power Off: 56mph

Standard Empty Weight: 1,902lb

Spray Tank Capacity: 151gal

Wing Span: 35ft, 10in

Length: 25ft, 9in

Height: 7ft, 9in

The AGtruck, showing the boom system below the wing with the dispersal pump between the wheels. The spray tank holds 280gal of chemicals.

a.m. It's still a way of making a living in an airplane that has freshly minted pilots lining up for a chance to go forth and lay spray on the land.

The Cessna AGcarryall serves in a multitude of ways. Being a modified C-185 with a 151gal spray tank hung underneath, it's not as limited as the single-seat airplanes. It makes for a good agricultural trainer. If you think about it, trying to learn how to dust in a single-seat airplane might be a little interesting, so having two seats, side by side, with all the dump controls mounted between the instructor and the student, is the only practical way to learn how to fly an agricultural airplane. The spray equipment can be easily removed, seats slid into place, and the Carryall can become a transport or cargo airplane in short order. Probably you'd want to give it a quick going over with some soap and water before you took the family to the Grand Canyon for the

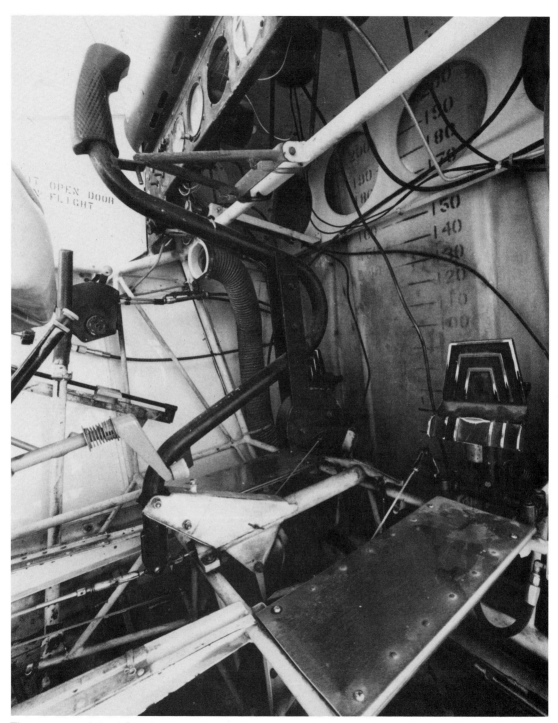

The operator of the AGtruck can easily see how many gallons of chemical remain in the tank. At 20ft off the ground and under power lines, the pilot probably doesn't spend a lot of time watching the liquid level.

Looks like an uncomfortable place to spend eight hot, sweaty hours, but the pilots I met all said they loved the job.

weekend. I don't think too many people would want to travel cross-country in a duster after a hard night's work, spraying defoliant. Might clash with the ladies' perfume. They do work hard, long hours, filled with stuff you would rather not have sloshing around on the cockpit floor with you. Given their original purpose in life, I'd imagine not too many AGcarryalls spend much time hauling people around on pleasure flights.

The AGwagon and AGtruck use the same airframe, same 300hp engine, same con-

trols, and same constant-speed prop. The main difference is the carrying capacity of each airplane. The AGwagon carries a 200gal tank, while the AGtruck is loaded with a heavier 280gal capacity. About the only way to tell them apart without reading the nameplate is to look for the fairings on the top of the strut on the AGtruck. Other than that, the wing on the AGtruck is 11.5in longer than that on the AGwagon, not something that stands out at 50ft above ground and 90mph.

Oh yeah, if I didn't mention it before, all the Cessna AGs are taildraggers, which adds a whole 'nother adventure to flying sprayers.

If you plan to make a career flying a Cessna AG airplane, it would behoove you to get a couple of hours of taildragger time in your logbook before showing up at someone's ag facility with hopes of employment. Say about 50 hours or so. The more, the merrier.

There are a number of ag pilot training courses advertised in the back of aviation magazines like Flying, offering ground school, flight time, and, in some cases, job placement. Most of them are located in the middle of the country, where the ground is flat and the horizon is filled with fields of wheat, so be prepared to relocate to a small airport in places like Idalia, Colorado, for the time it takes to learn how to dust down and dirty.

Cessna's not building new piston-engined agricultural airplanes anymore, and the people who have them tend to turn them over only after they have really earned their living. In buying a Cessna AG airplane, it's probably more important to have the airframe checked over by someone who works on the type for a living. Most of the airplanes up for sale have been maintained quite well, as the owners depend on them to make a liv-

Not exactly enough instruments for an IFR flight, but for spraying, it's all you need. The pilot's eyes are always out the window; instruments are for when you are taking off or landing. I've been told that if an AG pilot is real good, he can watch the ground with one eye, watch for wires with another and with what's left, scan the top four instruments while in a climbing turn.

ing. You can get away without servicing an airplane for a while, but when most of its time is spent within 50ft of the ground, flying slow and heavy, it's to your best advantage to make sure all the parts are in good condition. Not too many options when the engine sucks a valve as you go under the wires.

Occasionally the airplane goes through the wires instead of under them where it belongs. That's when you get to use the wire cutter bolted on the landing gear. Also most of the skills you have hopefully learned while flying dusters. Not that it happens very often, but if an agricultural plane goes twang in the wires, you want to make sure whoever checked it out afterwards made sure that any damage was repaired properly and entered in the logbook.

In general, when buying a duster, take someone who knows what it should be and have a good A&P mechanic go over it nut by bolt.

AG Plane Rating
Investment: #3
Utility: #1
Popularity: #2 (Bugs hate 'em; farmers love 'em.)

This prop is directly connected to the dispersal pump mounted under the belly of the AG plane. Everything you see under the plane looks like it works hard for a living. The spray bar is mounted directly behind the pump.

What a brand-new AG plane looked like before it had to earn its keep. *Cessna Aircraft Company*

Chapter 9

The Jets

Citation I, CitationJet, Citation 500, Citation V, and Citation SP

The original Citation was Cessna's answer to what you did when the old turboprop wasn't getting the job done fast enough. Cessna introduced the Citation 500 in 1972 as the first business-class jet that could compete with other turboprop aircraft then available.

It's certified for single-pilot operations, both VFR and IFR, day and night. Its strong suit has always been its ability to jump in and out of short runways, make economical, short hops, and generally do everything that a turboprop aircraft (such as the Beech King Air 200) could do, only with more go. The overall operating cost for a 1972 Citation 500, with a pair of Pratt & Whitney kerosene converters each pushing out 2,200lb of thrust, was down in the range of airplanes with propellers for motivation.

For another $100,000 ante over the cost of a King Air A-100, you can step right up with the big boys and go fly a jet to your next business meeting (Las Vegas, perhaps?). The Citation 500 and its newer editions will operate out of a 3,000ft strip without trouble and still go up to 37,000ft with 360kt to play with.

The Citation I S/P was introduced with serial number 0369 in 1977. It still had the same engines as the Citation 500, with a wing span 3ft longer on serial number 350 and up. This gave the S/P more performance up high and is reflected in the resale value of the indi-

vidual airplanes. The short-wing Citation usually brings $200,000 less than the later models. Expect to pay $1.2 million for a 1979 Citation I or S/P. The first year citation I or S/P will sell for $945,000 if equipped with thrust reversers on mid-time engines not past their second run on the turbine impellers. Expect to invest around $195,000 to $225,000 to have an engine overhauled and installed on any Citation 500 or S/P. TBO and rebuild costs are contingent on service bulletins, parts changes, and periodic inspections. Consider that the overhaul price could change in either direction as much as $40,000 depending on whether or not the impeller has to be replaced.

Cessna stretched the original 16ft-long cabin of the Citation I an additional 6.5ft to 22.6ft, changed the Pratt & Whitney 2500lb-thrust turbines to 2900lb-thrust engines, raised the takeoff weight to 15,900lb from the initial 10,000lb of the early jets, and called the resulting product the Citation V. Today a used 1989 model will bring $3.79 million, 100 percent of its retail price four years ago. All the newer serial numbers on the used jet market are also holding right at full retail, a condition that will probably hold true for the foreseeable future.

The Citation V cruises at 491mph with a climb to altitude time of 27 minutes to 41,000ft. A new wing with improved leading edge and flap designs contributes to the Cita-

Cessna CitationJet. Cessna reintroduces the entry level business jet, still capable of single-pilot oper- ation. If I was rich instead of a writer, I'd get in line for one of these.

tion V's superior performance at both ends of the flight envelope. The four-segment Fowler-type flaps extend inboard to the wing root, allowing lower approach speeds than do most turboprop aircraft. At sea level, on a 70-degree day with the flaps set at 15 degrees, the airplane will take off in less than 3,200ft. Given the same parameters, it can clear a 50ft obstacle and land in 2,870ft. You can flight plan for a crew of two and five passengers to use 3,400lb of fuel while covering 1,200nm nonstop. At a 420kt average cruise speed the flight will take three hours, portal to portal.

Right off the showroom floor, the Citation V comes equipped with the most com-

Cessna Citation II. This is the best-selling of all the business jets. It can be flown out of rough-surfaced runways and short fields and is capable of being configured for ten passengers at a 420mph cruise.

prehensive array of avionics ever offered as standard on this class of business jet. Most of the flight information will be scanned on Honeywell's two-tube Electronic Flight Instrument System (EFIS). The age of the video jet is upon us. This is quite a change from the first-generation solid-state technology found in the earlier Citations.

Cessna states that it determines year of the Citations by date of original airworthiness certificate, so you have to check the aircraft records to determine the year model of any particular aircraft that you are considering purchasing.

When I was a very, ever so really new pilot (no, airplanes didn't have to be hand-propped then), I took myself and my soon-to-be wife up to a favorite fly-in restaurant in

northern California called the Nut Tree. Runway length was 3,800ft. Since I had less than 25 hours on my ticket, all earned on San Jose International's runways (where the shortest was 4,400ft and 100ft wide), I was feeling real proud with myself for squeaking in a Cessna 172 on "only" 3,800ft of asphalt a measly 75ft wide. As I wandered off towards food, quietly drying my sweaty hands on my pants, two pilots dropped a Cessna Citation in on the runway, then turned off with about 1,000ft in front of them. I guess I still needed to put a few more hours in the logbook before American Airlines got a chance to put me in the left seat. The Citation pilot made it look easy, too! Probably did it every Saturday. Humbling. Sure impressed the wings right off my hat.

The largest of the straight wing Cessna jets, the Citation V. 16,000lb ramp weight, 7,110lb useful load and a 1,900-mile range with a 45,000ft ceiling.

The point being, a competent pilot in a Citation can run all over the country at a good rate of speed, while operating off runways that any self-respecting Lear Jet would give a pass. The Citation opened up many more small airports for jet travel.

Instead of taking something with propellers and chugging along at speeds in the 300mph range, you can run the Citation along, for a smaller fuel burn, at 420mph above the weather. You will put fewer hours on the engines for the same distance. And fewer hours mean lower yearly operating cost. Cessna says that a new Citation will push four people through the sky for as far as 1,725 miles for less than one dollar per mile. With its ability to leap out of fields as short as 2,960ft, you can get closer to your eventual destination than with other jets, so you spend less time going and more time being.

The original Citation 500 didn't really start out burning up the sky. With a cruise speed in the 325kt range, the aircraft suffered some derision from the boys in the Lears. Cessna responded in its usual way, by stretching the fuselage into the Citation V, an eleven-passenger jet capable of flying at 45,000ft while watching numbers like 425kt come up on the air speed indicator. After lengthening the body, uprating the engines, and generally changing almost every part on the basic 1972 Citation 500, Cessna dropped the short-bodied entry level model 501 in the early part of 1986.

Only recently did Cessna feel that the demand for an entry level jet was high enough to bring back the first Citation as the CitationJet. Cessna's marketing strategy is that the potential purchaser of a new CitationJet is someone who has been giving turboprops a close look. Rather than go head to head with its older Citation 500s and other models, Cessna has wisely elected to stress the affordability of purchase and economy of operation of a new, improved airplane.

Not every potential jet owner can afford to spend the money for a new kerosene burner. So what do you get when you go looking for a used Citation 500-series airplane? What kind of real world speeds and payload can you reasonably expect to carry?

First of all, you have to have a type rating in the airplane before you can take it out to play. If you are already instrument rated with a few hundred hours in twins, preferably with turbine time included, a type rating at a facility such as Flight Safety International will eat up most of $4,500 by the time you have logged hours as pilot in command. To keep your rating active, an annual check ride in the type of aircraft you hold a rating for and a twenty-four-month proficiency checkout in each specific aircraft you fly is required under FAA rules.

Probably no two Citations are currently flying that are exactly the same. Every cock-

Typical Citation Specifications
Engines, 1993: Rolls-Royce FJ 44 Turbofan of 1,900lb takeoff thrust with 3,500-hour TBO
Maximum Weight: 10,100lb, ramp; 10,000lb, takeoff
Fuel Capacity: 3,047lb
Maximum Cruise at 35,000ft and 8,500lb: 380kt
Range: 1,500nm
Rate of Climb: 3,540fpm; 1,070fpm single engine
Service Ceiling: 41,000ft; 26,200ft single engine
Takeoff Performance at 10,000lb: 2,960ft
Landing Performance at 9,500lb: 2,800ft over 50ft obstacle
Stall Speed at 10,000lb: 81kt
Standard Empty Weight (Operating): 6,430lb
Maximum Useful Load: 3,670lb
Maximum Useful Load with Full Fuel: 623lb
Wing Span: 45.2ft
Length: 42.6ft
Height: 13.7ft

pit will have some surprises for the potential buyer.

Avionics have changed so much in the last ten years that the possibility is high that any pre-1985 Citation 500 or SP will have had the panel massaged at least once. In an older, mid-70s, Model 500 without many upgrades, expect to find factory-original radios looking at you. Expect to have the pleasure of replacing the factory-original radios.

If the prior owner was a leasing or charter company, most of the time the early 400-series avionics will be uprated to Collins Pro-line or King Silver Crown equipment. Expect to see a panel with something along the lines of dual Collins navs and coms, ADF, radar altimeter, color radar by Sperry, HF radio, dual flight directors, VLF/Omega, and—if you live right—freon air conditioning in addition to the air cycle machine, to cool the greenhouse to livable levels.

Hopefully a complete intercom graces the panel, because the factory speakers left a lot to be desired and ten to fifteen years of baking inside an aluminum tube won't do much to improve already dubious sound quality. Actually, the Citation series are fairly quiet airplanes. If you have just stepped out of a twin with props spinning a few short feet from your ears, the sound levels will be much reduced. Not quite at the level of sitting in the easy chair at home, but a real change from anything with propellers. My last three years have been spent sandwiched between two 210hp Continentals with little or no insulation between them and my forty-eight-year-old ears. When I took off the headset at 28,000ft, I thought the engines had quit. After many years using the US Army's toys, shooting large-bore hunting rifles and flying loud warbirds, my low registers have long since retired. Or at least my wife says I must be two-thirds deaf, since I never seem to hear what she says. If I were rich instead of handsome, I'd probably never fly anything other than jets again.

Trying to cover what to look for in an airplane that has been crafted for at least 1,800 first-time owners and subsequent buyers would take a book of its own. Every airplane will reflect the prior owner's needs and wants. Best that you sit down with a lot of paper and figure out exactly what you need to see in a Citation before picking up the phone.

Just about everybody and their sister has some kind of modification for the Citation 500 series: gross weight increases, long wing conversions, fireblocked interior, freon air, recontour of the wing shape for reduced drag, thrust-reversers, new leather interiors, and trick paint. If you've got the money, someone

The cabin of the Citation V is 22.6ft long and almost 5ft wide. Still a bit like an upholstered aluminum tube, but with a dropped center aisle section, you can walk upright.

Similar to the older Citation III, the Citation VI is Cessna's affordable entry into the jet market. The III and the newer VI are still more expensive than buying a ticket on a commercial jet, but for corporate America, it's an efficient executive mover, and that's what counts.

will be happy to move it from your pocket to theirs in the process of uprating your Citation.

Speaking of money, (I know, I know—always talking about money) how much will a used Citation 500 or Citation SP reduce the balance in your Schwab account? You don't actually have to have a money market account or mutual funds at your disposal, but it sure will help when you go Citation hunting.

Something in a 1972 Citation 500, with the average amount of mods, will eat up

Same size as the Citation VI, the Citation VII will take you across the fruited plain at a maximum altitude of 51,000ft (higher than commercial flights) with all the modern conveniences that your corporation can buy. Will cover 2,300nm without a fuel stop.

Citation III Specifications
Engines: Garrett TFE731-3B-100S of 3,650lb thrust
Maximum Ramp Weight: 20,200lb
Maximum Performance: 467kt at 33,000ft
Range: 1,920nm, 4.3 hours with 7,155lb usable fuel and 1,750lb/hour
Rate of Climb: 4,340fpm; 1,285fpm single engine
Service Ceiling: 51,000ft; 28,150ft single engine
Takeoff Performance: 4,700ft
Landing Performance: 2,700ft over 50ft obstacle
Approach Speed with Flaps Down: 117kt
Stall Speed: 90kt
Number of Seats: 9–15
Maximum Useful Load: 9,249lb
Baggage: 800lb
Wingspan: 53ft, 6in
Length: 55ft, 6in
Height: 17ft, 3in

most of $500,000. To step into a 1979 Citation I/SP will lighten your bullion reserves by $100,000 plus change. You prefer a little newer, perhaps? I just happen to have a friend who is willing to part with the company 1985 Citation I SP 501 for $2.1 million. "Duck butter," you say. "I'll write the check."

While running around in the check-writing mode, one thing to bear in mind is maintenance records. And inspections. And ADs. The best of all possible worlds would be to find a Citation I with the wing mod, allowing you to go fly with just you in the airplane, all the current inspections up to date, updated avionics and low- to mid-time Pratt & Whitney engines with 3,500-hour TBOs stuck on the back. Sure you'll pay a premium for a good airplane. However, when dealing with jets, more so than with piston-engined airplanes, the inspection or AD that got skipped at the last annual could bring tears to your eyes and pain to your wallet.

If, on the other hand, you are contemplating buying a Citation and letting the old C-414 go out to pasture because your company's stock split again and the garage already has its quota of Bentley Continentals, plus the gun smiths at James Purdey & Sons Ltd. are running three years behind on their custom trap guns, you already own an FBO full of A&P mechanics who do nothing but work on Citations, you must be reading this book purely for its amusement value.

The other Citations based on the Model 500—the Citation I/SP, Citation II, and the current Citation V—are all transmuted versions of the first Model 500. More payload, more speed, better performance, more warm bodies on board, higher ceilings, more efficient Pratt & Whitney engines burning less fuel, excellent safety record. All part of the ongoing development of the Citation 500 that first blew out the door in 1972.

If you started in a 152, moved up to a 210, then flew one of Cessna's twins, flying a Citation I and its buddies will turn out to be an easy transition up the Cessna ladder. One wonders if they planned it that way?

Plus, you get the bonus of being able to drive the bus all by yourself, if the notion strikes.

Citation III, Citation VI, Citation VII

The Citation III and its newer brothers, the Citation VI and VII, are totally different airplanes from the first Citation 500s. The Citation III is a much larger jet with a high-aspect supercritical swept wing, upgraded fan-jet engines, and a lighter weight structure than most "mid-sized" business jets. Depending on how it's ordered, the Citation III can be equipped with low-density seating for nine people or high-density seating for fifteen. Fill the tanks, put six people on board, and take them in comfort at more than 500mph across the continent—or across the ocean.

Citation VI and VII Specifications

Engines, Citation VI: Garrett TFE731-3B-100S of 3,650lb thrust
Engines, Citation VII: Garrett TFE731-4R-2S of 4,000lb thrust
Maximum Weight, Citation VI: 22,000lb
Maximum Weight, Citation VII: 22,450lb
Maximum Cruise Speed, Citation VI: 473kt at 37,000ft
Maximum Cruise Speed, Citation VII: 478kt at 37,000ft
Maximum Range, Citation VI: 2,345nm
Maximum Range, Citation VII: 2,300nm
Rate of Climb at Sea Level, Citation VI: 3,699fpm
Rate of Climb at Sea Level, Citation VII: 4,000fpm
Takeoff Runway Length, Citation VI: 5,150ft
Takeoff Runway Length, Citation VII: 4,940ft
Landing Runway Length, Citation VI: 2,900ft
Landing Runway Length, Citation VII: 3,000ft
Standard Empty Weight, Citation VI: 12,775lb
Standard Empty Weight, Citation VII: 11,686lb
Useful Load, Citation VI: 9,425lb
Useful Load, Citation VII: 10,964lb
Length: 55.5ft
Width: 53.5ft
Height: 16.8ft

The newer VI (introduced in 1991) and VII (introduced in 1992) are certified to fly at 51,000ft, bypassing all the bumps and grinds of weather. Very important to know that the drinks won't spill on the pants leg of a CEO you're trying to sell on the idea of buying your company.

Few, if any, of the bigger Citations are owned by a single person. Usually the bean-counters, buried in the dark sub-basement, are the driving force in how much money gets spent on what kind of go-fast. Most of the owners are real familiar with the Fortune 500 companies. When you drop $4.3 million on a 1984 Citation III, it helps to have the monetary power of a large company behind you.

Most people pick a jet the size of the Citation III to transport people whose time is more valuable than the money saved by flying the scheduled airlines. The jets are seen as airborne offices, replete with all the modern conveniences that enable business to be conducted in high places. Whether it's a phone call to a company three states away, a real-time stock quotation, or a business meeting for four, the Citation can be equipped to cover it all.

Cessna has screwed together over 200 Citation IIIs that have gone to all corners of the world. Those jets have logged over 200 million miles of flying in every imaginable field of service. The resale value of a five-to-six-year-old Citation III is better than any other aircraft in its class. Most of the Citation IIIs coming on the used-jet market are equipped with more avionics than the Boeing 747s of a decade past. Judging from the cockpits (excuse me—flight decks) I've seen, the newer models come with everything except turn signals.

And the back end of the airplane wasn't exactly Spartan, either. The occupants had to make do with only seven leather seats in the interior, a custom galley sporting a microwave oven, a CD player, and a cassette video with multiple monitors. How the rich must suffer! My 182 didn't even come with a black-and-white TV. I even saw a 1980s Citation III with a 24-carat gold-plated interior, TV, VCR, Airshow, full galley, extended wine rack, and more. I think it even flew, too.

I don't really know how I would point you at one Citation in lieu of another. All the aircraft, if maintained properly, will return excellent performance for the dollar. As you have seen, almost every one is slightly different. With an options list slightly smaller than a New York City phone directory, the choices are endless. I suppose one could hang enough bits and pieces on one of these planes that it would turn into a two-passenger jet, if so desired.

How to pick one? Figure out the missions it will fly, the budget to operate it, the initial affordable cost. Then look up a company that specializes in pre-owned Citations, like Cessna ValuePlus, and send 'em a fax for a listing.

Citation X

I thought this .9 Mach business jet at least deserved to be mentioned. It's quite possible that finding a used one might take a bit of work, since Cessna doesn't expect to have any of them flying until 1995.

But for those of you who can't wait for anything, especially a new go-fast airplane, here's a tidbit or two.

Planned as the fastest business jet in the world, the Citation X is expected to be able to shoot from New York to London in under seven hours. The boys and girls at Cessna are going to hang two GM/Allison smokers, flat-rated to 6,000lb of thrust per engine on the back, so the jet actually might turn out to be that fast, if not faster. The cabin interior will be 6ft longer than the interior of mid-size Citations. What it doesn't have, for goodies in the cabin or avionics on the flight deck, doesn't exist. Everything about the airplane will be super-trick, including the price. Should be able to beat Cessna out of one for just a little over $14 million.

If this sounds good, go give Citation marketing a call at 1-800-4-Cessna; they're waiting for your call.

I think we've come a long way from my 1955 Cessna 180. And I don't think we're ever going back!

Coming soon to a dealer near you, the Citation X. The fastest business jet ever built: 594mph with a five-year, 2,500hr warranty on the engines. The ultimate cross-country airplane.

Useful Addresses

Baja Bush Pilots
P.O. Box 34280
San Diego, CA 92163

Cessna Airmaster Club
9 South 135 Aero Drive
Naperville, IL 60565

Cessna Owner Organization
P.O. Box 337
Iola, WI 54945

Cessna Pilots Association
P.O. Box 12948
Wichita, KS 67277

Cessna T-50 Flying Bobcats
3821 53rd Street S.E.
Auburn, WA 98002

Cessna Tech Center
3409 Corsair Circle
Santa Maria, CA 93455

FAA
US Department of Transportation
Aviation Standards National Field Office
Examinations Standards Branch, AVN-130
P.O. Box 25082
Oklahoma City, OK 73125

International Bird Dog Association
3939 C-8 San Pedro, N.E.
Albuquerque, NM 87110

International Cessna 120/140 Association
6425 Hazelwood Avenue
Northfield, MN 55057

Trade-A-Plane
410 West Fourth Street
Crossville, TN 38557

Index